The Spanish-American War

The Story and Photographs

Selected Titles by the Authors

By Donald M. Goldstein and Katherine V. Dillon:
  Amelia: The Centennial Biography of an Aviation Pioneer (1997)
  The Pearl Harbor Papers: Inside the Japanese Plans (1993)
  The Williwaw War (1992)
By Donald M. Goldstein, Katherine V. Dillon, and J. Michael Wenger:
  The Vietnam War: The Story and Photographs (1997)
  Rain of Ruin: A Photographic History of Hiroshima and Nagasaki (1995)
  "Nuts!": The Battle of the Bulge (1994)
  D-Day Normandy: The Story and Photographs (1993)
  The Way It Was: Pearl Harbor—The Original Photographs (1991)
By Gordon W. Prange, Donald M. Goldstein, and Katherine V. Dillon:
  God's Samurai: Lead Pilot at Pearl Harbor (1990)
  December 7, 1941: The Day the Japanese Attacked Pearl Harbor (1988)
  Pearl Harbor: The Verdict of History (1987)
  Target Tokyo: The Story of the Sorge Spy Ring (1984)
  Miracle at Midway (1982)
  At Dawn We Slept: The Untold Story of Pearl Harbor (1981)
By Donald M. Goldstein, Katherine V. Dillon, and Masataka Chihaya:
  Fading Victory: The Diary of Admiral Matome Ugaki (1991)
By J. Michael Wenger and Robert J. Cressman:
  Infamous Day: Marines at Pearl Harbor, 7 December 1941 (1992)
  Steady Nerves and Stout Hearts: The Enterprise *(CV-6) Air Group and Pearl Harbor,
    7 December 1941* (1990)
By Donald M. Goldstein, Phil Williams, and J.M. Shafritz:
  Classic Readings of International Relations (1994)
By Donald M. Goldstein, Phil Williams, and Hank Andrews:
  Security in Korea: War, Stalemate and Negotiation (1994)
By Robert J. Cressman:
  "A Magnificent Fight": The Battle for Wake Island (1995)
  That Gallant Ship: USS Yorktown *(CV-5)* (1985)
By Robert J. Cressman, Steve Ewing, Barrett Tillman, Mark Horan, Clark Reynolds, and Stan Cohen:
  "A Glorious Page in Our History," The Battle of Midway, 4–6 June 1942 (1990)

The Spanish-American War

The Story and Photographs

BY

DONALD M. GOLDSTEIN

KATHERINE V. DILLON

J. MICHAEL WENGER

AND

ROBERT J. CRESSMAN

BRASSEY'S

WASHINGTON • LONDON

Editorial Offices:
22883 Quicksilver Drive
Dulles, VA 20166

Order Department:
P.O. Box 960
Herndon, VA 20172

Brassey's books are available at special discounts for bulk purchases for sales promotions, premiums, fund-raising, or educational use.

Library of Congress Cataloging-in-Publication Data

The Spanish-American War: the story and photographs / by Donald M.
    Goldstein…[et al.].—Centennial ed.
        p.   cm.
    Includes bibliographical references and index.
    ISBN 1-57488-076-4
    1. Spanish American War, 1898—Pictorial works.   2. Spanish-
American war, 1898.   I. Goldstein, Donald M.
    E715.S79   1998
    973.8´9—dc21   98-16363
                                                                        CIP

First Edition

Book design by Page Graphics, Inc.

10   9   8   7   6   5   4   3   2   1

Printed in the United States of America

Contents

An AUSA
Institute of Land Warfare
Book

The Association of the United States Army, or AUSA, was founded in 1950 as a nonprofit organization dedicated to education concerning the role of the U.S. Army, to providing material for military professional development, and to the promotion of proper recognition and appreciation of the profession of arms. Its constituencies include those who serve in the Army today, including Army National Guard, Army Reserve, and Army civilians, the retirees and veterans who have served in the past, and all their families. A large number of public-minded citizens and business leaders are also an important constituency. The Association seeks to educate the public, elected and appointed officials, and leaders of the defense industry on crucial issues involving the adequacy of our national defense, particularly those issues affecting land warfare.

In 1988, AUSA established within its existing organization a new entity known as the Institute of Land Warfare. ILW's mission is to extend the educational work of AUSA by sponsoring a wide range of publications, to include books, monographs, and essays on key defense issues, as well as workshops, symposia, and since 1992, a television series. Among the volumes chosen as "An AUSA Institute of Land Warfare Book" are both new texts and reprints of titles of enduring value. Topics include history, policy issues, strategy, and tactics. Publication as an AUSA Book does not indicate that the Association of the United States Army and the publisher agree with everything in the book but does suggest that AUSA and the publisher believe the book will stimulate the thinking of AUSA members and others concerned about important defense-related issues.

Preface

This volume is unique among those of this series of military histories in that the authors did not live through the period and thus have no direct personal experience of either the events on the scene or the reactions of the U.S. population. There was, however, sufficient source material to make the project possible and enjoyable.

Chapter 1 briefly describes Cuba and its people in 1898, events and individuals behind that land's drive for freedom, the sinking of the battleship *Maine*, and the subsequent rupture of relations between Spain and the United States. In Chapter 2, the United States raises an army, establishes camps, and prepares to fight. Chapter 3 gives brief sketches of the most important individuals involved. Chapter 4 describes the arms and ships involved, a much shorter list than for later wars.

Chapter 5 tells of Commodore George Dewey's spectacular victory at Manila Bay in the Philippines. Chapter 6 deals with early U.S. action in Cuba, including the *Merrimac* incident and the landing of U.S. Marines at Guantánamo. In Chapter 7 the newly-organized U.S. troops sail for Cuba with considerable confusion and difficulty, make their early landings in Cuba, and engage in the battle of Las Guásimas.

Chapter 8 describes three major engagements of the Cuban land campaign—El Caney, Kettle Hill, and San Juan Hill, the latter to be linked forever with the name Theodore Roosevelt. Chapter 9 deals with the naval battle off Santiago, which destroyed Admiral Pascual Cervera y Topete's Spanish squadron in Cuban waters. Chapter 10 returns to land, the final action at Santiago, the alarming increase in disease, and the surrender of General José Vasquez Toral's command. Chapter 11 describes the situation in Cuba at the end of hostilities, the beginning of troop returns to the United States and of the Spanish soldiers to their homeland, the taking of Puerto Rico, and the final

victory in the Philippines, with the formal peace between Spain and the United States. Chapter 12 describes some of the memorials erected, ships salvaged, and the recovery and disposal of the wreckage of the *Maine*. It also briefly describes the Philippine insurrection and the consequences of the war.

Many photographs are available from the Spanish-American War period, but in general they are in no better, and frequently worse, condition than those taken during the Civil War because the hot and humid Cuban climate was detrimental to plates and delicate camera equipment. Few, if any, developers were worried about altering the negatives. While the fleet had no official photographers on board, a few amateur shutterbugs served on some of the ships. Most likely, however, such artists as Frederic Remington and Howard Chandler Christy left the best and, in spirit at least, the truest pictorial account of the conflict.

All the photographs in this book are from the National Archives, the Naval Historical Center, or the authors' collections. All are in the public domain, and the authors have copies of them on file for reference. Dr. Jeffrey G. Barlow kindly allowed the authors to use two pictures from his personal collection.

Useful works to the student of the Spanish-American War are David P. Trask's *The War with Spain in 1898* (1981), Graham A. Cosmas's *An Army for Empire: The United States Army in the Spanish-American War* (1971), John L. Offner's *An Unwanted War: The Diplomacy of the United States and Spain over Cuba, 1895–1898* (1992), Frank Friedel's *The Splendid Little War* (1958), and French E. Chadwick's *The Relations of the United States and Spain: The Spanish-American War* (1911). Hyman G. Rickover's *How the* Maine *Was Destroyed* (1970) and Peggy and Harold Samuels's *Remembering the* Maine (1995) present thought-provoking analyses of that disaster. Useful in their contemporary reflection of the times are Trumbull White's *Pictorial History of Our War with Spain* (1898) and Henry Watterson's *History of the Spanish-American War* (1898). *The Campaign of Santiago de Cuba*, a three-volume work by Herbert H. Sargent published in 1907 and based on official reports, remains an invaluable source of detail on the Cuban campaign.

We would like to thank all those at the Still Pictures Branch of the National Archives, College Park, Maryland, and at the Curator Branch, Photographic Section of the Naval Historical Center, Washington, D.C., as well as Dr. Jeffrey G. Barlow for his contribution; F. Patterson Anthony, Michael Rachlin, and Donald C. Mellen for their help in understanding period ordnance; Jim Sutton and Don McKeon at Brassey's for their support and encouragement; and Leah Campos, Doug Brooks, Rob Mullin, and Chris Dishman for their assistance. A special thanks goes to Sheila Kelly and Kendall Stanley for their typing and editorial assistance.

We dedicate this book to the memory of those who fought and died on both sides of this conflict.

DONALD M. GOLDSTEIN, Ph.D.
Professor, Public and International Affairs
University of Pittsburgh
Pittsburgh, Pa.

KATHERINE V. DILLON
CWO USAF (Ret.)
Arlington, Va.

J. MICHAEL WENGER, M.A.
Raleigh, N.C.

ROBERT J. CRESSMAN, M.A.
Rockville, Md.

Introduction

On the surface, the late 1890s appeared to be a serene—indeed, rather dull—period in American history. The Civil War was far enough in the past that the wounds were healing, the economy was prosperous, and Native Americans were no longer a menace. One could travel from the East Coast to the West, although neither rapidly nor comfortably. It has been postulated that the country was suffering from national claustrophobia because, in Stephen Vincent Benét's poignant phrase, "there was no longer any west." For more than 250 years this had been a nation of pioneers. Now that the natural borders had been reached, this theory continued, it was only to be expected that Americans should look beyond the seas. On the other hand, there was an opposing philosophy: that this was it, this was our natural homeland, still with plenty of room.

"But," said the social Darwinists, "it is your duty to move beyond your borders. The Lord in His wisdom has made you white, northern European, literate, monogamous and hardworking. Obviously you are superior to those who are none of these things, so you are destined to take over their territory, rule them, and operate their resources for their—and your—benefit."

A surprising number of Americans, although not so serenely self-confident and self-satisfied as the British, accepted social Darwinism. Fortunately, for most this arrogant concept was softened by a genuine, if rather patronizing, kindliness. President William McKinley's famous comment about the Philippines, addressed to a group of Methodist clergymen on November 21, 1899, exemplified this attitude: "There was nothing left for us to do but take them all, and to educate the Filipinos, and uplift and civilize and Christianize them, and by God's grace do the very best we could by them, as our fellow-men for whom Christ also died."

Another enormously potent theory was expounded by Alfred Thayer Mahan, who particularized his thesis of the influence of sea power to specify the United States. As her production increased, she would require overseas markets; access to overseas markets would demand a large merchant marine; to protect her merchant marine, the United States would need a large navy; a large navy would require shipyards and coaling stations, which meant colonies that in turn could help support the entire cycle.

Theodore Roosevelt was one of Mahan's most enthusiastic advocates. Indeed, Roosevelt might be considered the personification of the age, its strengths and its weaknesses. Well-born, well-educated, a distinguished writer, he felt obligated to enter public service. He did so, however, not only from duty but also from a burning ambition. He was an ideal family man—affectionate, interested, good-humored; he was also belligerently macho and embraced war as evidence of a healthy national virility. He was by no means alone in that attitude and, to do him justice, he was ready, indeed eager, to put himself in harm's way.

These various philosophies simmered in the American consciousness, but no one knows what directions they might have taken if left to develop naturally. William Randolph Hearst and other press moguls wanted to sell newspapers and therefore agitated public opinion over the situation in Cuba, which indeed was deplorable. At one time, Spain had controlled much of South and Central America and large sections of North America, but by the 1890s Spain possessed only Cuba and Puerto Rico in the Western Hemisphere and the Philippines and the Ladrones in the Eastern.

The Americans were little concerned about the Ladrones, and many well-educated people would have had difficulty locating the Philippines geographically. Cuba, however, was another matter; it was practically next door. Cuban insurgents had been fighting the Spanish authorities for years, but neither side could score a real victory. Spain had made concessions to Cuba, but by that time the Cubans did not want concessions, they wanted independence.

The "yellow press" in the United States reported every incident of Spanish oppression, real or imaginary, and whipped up indignation in the United States. Misunderstandings existed on both sides. Some Europeans had only vague notions about the United States. Asked what strategy he would advise against the Americans, a Spanish admiral is said to have replied confidently, "I should advise the sending of a fleet against Washington first; then after reducing the city, the fleet should proceed to Chicago and bring it to terms." A French naval captain who assured his readers that "Cuba is not far from Havana" located the Philippines in the Indian Ocean and the Canary Islands in the China Sea.

Those in charge in Madrid, however, entertained no such wild notions and were exceedingly anxious to have no trouble with the United States as long as the ever-central "honor" of Spain was maintained. How long the gradual buildup of ill will might have continued to escalate is questionable, but Fate took a hand. The battleship *Maine* exploded in Havana harbor. The yellow press pulled out all the stops, and, in general, U.S. public opinion accepted that the Spanish had deliberately blown up *Maine*. Recent investigations indicate that while the occurrence was probably an accident, the possibility of a desperate step by parties who stood to benefit from such an act cannot be discounted. Some may still believe that Spain was responsible, but the Spanish were not fools: their country was almost bankrupt and was divided politically. The last thing the Spanish would have done was deliberately sink an American battleship.

Thus, the United States declared war on Spain, defeated her soundly in record time, and ended up liking and respecting their former enemy considerably more than their erstwhile allies, the Cuban and Filipino insurgents. In a way, Spain profited from her defeat. She had gotten rid of a no longer viable empire and was able to concentrate her efforts on the home country. In contrast, the United States stepped onto the international stage in a hitherto unthought-of role, one in which she was not entirely comfortable. Pacifying the Philippines took much longer than it had taken to overcome Spain and left many Americans with an uneasy conscience. Within fifty years of conquest, the United States granted Philippine independence and would have done so sooner had not World War II intervened. Cuba was a protectorate for a relatively short time. Puerto Rico and Guam seem to be well satisfied under the American flag. One other piece of territory came into American possession indirectly through the Spanish-American War—Hawaii.

The Spanish-American War period acted as a bridge between America's past and future. As one reads the accounts, one catches glimpses of the past in the form of names familiar from the Civil War. Then, with a shock of recognition, one encounters a name that would be prominent in World War I or II. For a while there was a tendency to treat the Spanish-American War as a sort of opéra bouffe conflict or a rather amusing incident. There is nothing amusing about any war, with its attendant death, injury, destruction, and heartbreak. We hope this account, with its photographs, will make the Spanish-American War come alive for readers with a brief reflection of how it was in 1898.

The Cuban Situation

Early Spanish accounts agree that the natives of the island that Christopher Columbus named Juana when he visited it on October 28, 1492, were gentle, courteous, and hospitable. By the late nineteenth century, however, it would have been difficult, if not impossible, to find any trace of the native culture except in the name of the country. The island had gone through a series of name changes, and eventually officials settled on Cuba, short for Cubanacan.

In the Cuba of 1898, Cubans were divided ethnically into three groups: those of Spanish descent, who were considered white (1-1); those of mixed blood and mulattoes, many of whom also were considered white (1-2); and descendants of Africans who had been brought to the New World as slaves (1-3).

Although Cuba was predominantly rural, a number of large cities flourished. Second only in importance and size to the capital of Havana was the

1-1 Two *señoritas* pose for a photographer on a balcony overlooking the courtyard of the Gran Hotel at Puerto Príncipe.

1-2 Cuban natives of mixed blood gather in front of a hut in Cabaignon for photographer E. C. Rost, who accompanied the U.S. Army in Cuba.

1-3 *Reconcentrados*, black victims of Weyler's policies directed against the insurgents, stare at Rost near one of the Cuban civil hospitals.

busy port of Santiago (1-4), located on the southeast coast north of the island of Jamaica. Santiago initially played no important part in American war plans, which concentrated on Havana.

Although a substantial city by any measure, Santiago retained a provincial, small-town flavor (1-5). Central to the life of the city was the large city market (1-6), where the citizens could supply their needs and hear the latest news and rumors. Religion (1-7) provided another unifying element for the citizens. Despite these colorful and impressive aspects of Cuban life, it was impossible to ignore certain harsh realities, including the poor sanitary conditions that prevailed across the island, even in the larger cities (1-8).

No city of Spanish culture was without its bullring (1-9 and 1-10). Other popular pastimes were cockfighting and a curious game called goose-grabbing, in which the declared winner was the first mounted rider to snatch the head off a goose tied down to the road. Americans recoiled with disgust when they first witnessed such spectacles. The perceived cruelty of the Cubans, not only to animals but toward their own kind, somewhat cooled the liberating ardor of the American troops.

1-4 The port of Santiago

1-5 Street scene near the wharf in Santiago

1-6 Marina Calle (Marina Street), showing the city market

1-7 Church of Santa Lucia

1-8 San Felix Calle, with raw sewage coursing down the middle of the thoroughfare

1-9 Santiago's bullfight arena, on the north-eastern outskirts of the city

1-10 Interior of the bullring

Santiago, however, was atypical of Cuba. More representative were the small towns such as Sancti Spiritus, with its stone bridge and ubiquitous palm trees (1-11).

Havana, Cuba's largest city and its capital, was in a class by itself with its mixture of squalor and magnificence. An example of the former was Havana harbor (1-12) in the 1890s. Into it emptied all the sewage of the city, and no freshwater stream entered it to purify the water, nor was there much tidal movement. This was a prime example of Spanish mismanagement and indifference, because to correct the situation required only a simple and relatively inexpensive matter of engineering.

Outside the port area, matters improved. Streets were cobbled, although there were few sidewalks wide enough to accommodate more

1-11 The small town of Sancti Spiritus

1-12 The port of Havana, Cuba's capital and largest city

than two abreast. On the other hand, some streets were lined with specialty shops whose wares would not have disgraced Paris. Havana also boasted many impressive official structures (1-13). Homes of the upper classes were designed primarily to combat the heat: windows had no glass and doors were usually left ajar.

The casual traveler who delved no deeper could readily have pigeonholed Cuba in the 1890s as a semitropical place of indolent good nature where nothing much ever happened. But beneath the surface, tensions had been building for years.

Affairs in Cuba had concerned Americans well before relations between the United States and Spain reached a critical point in 1898, most notably when the *Virginius* incident brought the two countries to the brink of war a quarter of a century before. The crisis centered around the side-wheel steamer *Virginius*, which had been purchased from the United States by Cuban interests to transport war matériel to the insurgents in Cuba. The former Civil War blockade runner had acquired a notorious reputation as a filibuster that on occasion flew the Stars and Stripes as a flag of convenience.

1-13 Residence of the captain general in Havana.

1-14 Cubans reenact the atrocity at Alemenda Wall outside Santiago where the Spanish shot the *Virginius* prisoners.

On October 31, 1873, the Spanish corvette *Tornado* captured the *Virginius* off the coast of Jamaica, took her 52 crewmen and 103 passengers—16 Americans and 9 Britons among them—prisoner, and transported them to Santiago, where General Don Juan de Burriel, commanding the military district headquartered there, treated them as pirates (1-14). Burriel refused American vice consul Emil G. Schmitt access to those who claimed protection under the U.S. flag and denied him use of the telegraph so that he was unable to learn from the U.S. consul at Kingston, Jamaica, whether the *Virginius* had cleared that port under American papers. On the strength of an 1869 edict and without consulting with either Havana or Madrid, Burriel, after a "drum-head court martial," ordered the prisoners executed. A firing squad shot the first four, including a Canadian soldier of fortune who had thrown in his lot with the insurgents, on November 4.

While Vice Consul Schmitt tried to obtain an audience with Burriel and officials in Washington, D.C., sought more information, the concern over the *Virginius*'s capture and the possible detention of English subjects prompted the British to send the sloop HMS *Niobe* to Santiago. In the meantime, hearing of *Niobe*'s departure, Burriel advanced the date of the execution by one day and,

on November 7, had Capt. Joseph Fry, an American, the *Virginius*'s master, and thirty-six other men (seven of whom were Americans) shot. Twelve more men taken from the *Virginius*, all Cubans, died before a firing squad on November 8.

Burriel's butchery did not escape condemnation in Cuba; members of Santiago's clergy asked the general to stop the executions. Appeals for mercy, however, paled before the application of brute force: *Niobe*'s arrival in Santiago on the afternoon of November 8 proved a threat to be reckoned with, as Cmdr. Sir Lambton Loraine, Royal Navy, the warship's captain, accompanied the British vice consul to lodge a protest with Burriel. Not wanting to beard the British lion, Burriel assured his visitors that there would be no more executions that day. The arrival at Santiago soon thereafter of American warships reflected U.S. concern.

Eventually, the crisis came to an end; an investigation proved the fraudulent nature of the *Virginius*'s "American" registry, and Spanish authorities in Cuba returned the survivors to the custody of the U.S. Navy sloop *Juniata* in early December. Spain formally apologized and paid an indemnity to the families of the slain Americans.

America was preoccupied with domestic affairs at the time, however, such as the panic of 1873, and was not in the mood for war. This was perhaps fortunate for the United States, for neither the U.S. Navy nor the U.S. Army was a match for the Spanish in 1873.

During the years between the *Virginius* incident and the outbreak of the Spanish-American War, Cuba writhed in a state of constant turmoil. Outright war between the Spanish and the Cuban insurgents, the Ten Years' War, had raged from 1868 to 1878, ending in a precarious peace that solved nothing. Every concession the Spanish made was effectively frustrated by limiting rules and regulations. Why did Spain try so stubbornly to keep and subdue Cuba? The island had never been a major source of profit, and by the 1890s Spain was operating Cuba in the red. The "ever-faithful isle" had become a liability rather than an asset. The instinct to keep control of Spain's last shred of her American empire, however, seemed to overcome any considerations of logic.

As the crisis drew nearer, three extraordinary men arose to lead and strengthen the Cuban insurgent movement. The first of these was José Julián Martí y Pérez, the son of a Spanish soldier, whose earliest lessons presumably would have been loyalty to the faraway motherland. At school, however, he came under the influence of a teacher who believed in democracy in the abstract and Cuban independence in the concrete. By the age of fifteen Martí was committed to these principles and remained so all his life. He had a fine mind and was an excellent writer; probably he could have enjoyed a lasting reputation as an author. As it was, one of his plays, however, earned him two years in prison and exile in Spain. While there, he earned a college degree, made a number of converts to Cuba's cause, and then moved to Mexico. When the Ten Years' War ended and political exiles were pardoned, he returned to Cuba.

In less than a year, he was exiled again, this time to New York City. He lived there for seventeen years, working tirelessly for Cuba's independence with such fellow exiles as Máximo Gómez y Báez (1-15) and Antonio Maceo y Grajales (1-16). On February 24, 1895, he summoned his countrymen to arise. He and Gómez landed in Cuba at Cobonico on April 14, 1895. Martí's presence infused new life into the cause and new recruits flocked to join him. Named a major general, he led several successful minor engagements; he was killed on May 19, 1895, in battle at Dos Rios.

1-15 Maj. Gen. Máximo Gómez y Báez, general-in-chief and leader of the Cuban insurgents

1-16 Maj. Gen. Antonio Maceo y Grajales, Gómez's second in command

The loss of this charismatic leader was a blow, but he was ably succeeded by Máximo Gómez y Báez. Like Martí, Gómez was a man of education and intelligence, but unlike Martí, he was primarily a soldier, having served in the Spanish army. Fearing that if he remained in the Spanish army, he eventually would have to fight his Cuban countrymen, however, he resigned. He then participated in the Ten Years' War and at its end in 1878 retired to his birthplace, Santo Domingo in the Dominican Republic. On a visit to the United States, he joined Martí's group of expatriates but then returned to Santo Domingo. In 1895 Martí selected Gómez commander of the insurgent forces, and Gómez accepted. He proved to be a master of guerrilla warfare, with which General Valeriano Weyler y Nicolau's regulars were unable to cope physically or psychologically. Gómez's defiance of the hated Weyler and his refusal to accept the compromise of autonomy won Gómez and his cause many admirers in the United States.

Gómez's second in command was Maj. Gen. Antonio Maceo Grajales, a mulatto of keen mind, great military skill, and strict moral character. Like William McKinley, he neither played cards, smoked, nor drank and would not have heavy drinkers about him. Standing some five feet ten inches—quite tall by Cuban standards—with unusually broad shoulders, he was a picturesque figure, sporting a pearl-handled .38 revolver and a Toledo blade shaped like a machete. In civilian life a fastidious dresser, he always "roughed it" with his men, winning their undying devotion. Maceo's guerrillas were unusual in that they were mounted, and fine riders.

Weyler was particularly eager to get rid of Maceo, partly from racial pride, but primarily because Maceo and his men were adept at destroying such sources of Spanish revenue as sugar fields and mills. What the Spanish could not do in battle they accomplished through treachery. Maceo's physician and friend, Doctor Zertucha, betrayed Maceo to Spanish bushwackers, who killed him in December 1896. As they had after Martí's death, the Spanish assumed that the loss of

Maceo would take the heart out of the revolution. Instead, it aroused the insurgents to even stronger determination.

In that same year, 1896, President Grover Cleveland appointed as consul to Havana a distinguished Virginian, Fitzhugh Lee (1-17). Because Cuba was not yet an independent nation, the United States had no embassy there, so the post of consul in Havana was more significant than it was in other nations. When McKinley became president, he retained Lee in the position. Lee, a nephew of Robert E. Lee, was, like his distinguished relative, a West Pointer. He was well on the way to a solid career in the U.S. Army when the Civil War broke out. He resigned his commission, joined the Confederate Army, served well in the cavalry, and received a promotion to major general in 1863. After the war he retired for several years to the life of a country gentleman, although he was active in Confederate veterans' groups and in reconciling the former foes. In 1885 he became governor of Virginia for one term. In 1896 came his appointment to Havana.

Lee gathered and forwarded to Washington much valuable information about the explosive situation in Cuba. Initially, he favored the insurgents' cause and urged that the United States intervene. Later he modified his stand, and on January 24, 1898, requested that Washington not

1-17 Fitzhugh Lee, American consul general in Havana

send a warship to Havana. The battleship *Maine*, however, had already sailed that day.

Riots in Cuba on January 12 had played a part in the U.S. government's decision to send a warship to Cuba, resuming the regular calls to Cuban ports that had been discontinued during Cleveland's administration. The choice had fallen upon *Maine*, commissioned on September 17, 1895 (1-18). She displaced 6,682 tons and carried a main battery of four 10-inch/.35-caliber breech-loading rifles (BLRs) and a secondary battery of six 6-inch/.40-caliber BLRs. *Maine*'s commanding officer, Capt. Charles D. Sigsbee, wrote to his wife that his command was the "chosen of the flock" to

represent the United States in Havana at that tense time.

Maine, however, was not the only U.S. warship in Cuban waters at the time; the unprotected cruiser* *Montgomery* (1-19) visited Matanzas and Santiago during February 1898. Local conditions profoundly shocked *Montgomery*'s skipper, Cmdr. George A. Converse (1-20). On February 6, 1898,

_____

*"Protected cruisers" had an armored deck to protect their vitals (but no side armor) and main batteries of 8-inch guns or 6-inch guns. Unprotected cruisers had no armor protection and a main battery of 5-inch guns; in fact, they were actually large gunboats.

1-18 The U.S. battleship *Maine* stands in to Havana harbor, January 25, 1898.

1-20 Cmdr. George A. Converse, *Montgomery*'s commanding officer

1-19 The unprotected cruiser *Montgomery* in the mid-1890s

he reported that the "distress [in Matanzas] was no longer confined to . . . the laboring country people, most of whom have already perished . . . but has now extended to the upper classes, who before the war were in moderately comfortable circumstances." Converse reported that clamoring crowds of starving men, women, and children followed *Montgomery*'s officers whenever they landed, begging them for food. "The urgent necessity of immediate relief," he declared, "can not be exaggerated." The situation at Santiago, he wrote on February 12, was "not nearly as great as at Matanzas."

Meanwhile, Captain Sigsbee on board *Maine* was having a comparatively placid time of it. The Spanish authorities had been correct, if not cor-

dial, and Sigsbee had met with a number of local notables (1-21). The visit was proceeding with "no appreciable excitement." On February 13, *Maine*'s officers entertained at lunch Miss Clara Barton (1-22), who had recently arrived with a group of Red Cross people to try to alleviate the suffering of the *reconcentrados*, rural Cubans who had been forced into concentration camps by the Spanish to prevent them from providing support for the Cuban rebels. She contrasted "those polished tables, the glittering china and cut glass" with the terrible privations her new charges were enduring.

Two days later, *Maine* rode peacefully at her moorings on what promised to be another tranquil day (1-23). Taps sounded at 8:45 P.M., and, other than the officers and men on watch at their

1-21 Consul Fitzhugh Lee (center) sits with Capt. Charles D. Sigsbee, commanding officer of the battleship *Maine*, an unidentified civilian, and Lt. Friend W. Jenkins, one of *Maine*'s junior officers, on board a steamer in Havana harbor. Sigsbee survived the destruction of his ship; Jenkins did not.

1-22 Clara Barton, famed Red Cross nurse

1-23 *Maine* moored in Havana harbor at 4:00 P.M. on February 15, 1898.

posts, most of her complement had turned in. A few officers lingered in the wardroom. In his cabin, Sigsbee was "just closing a letter to his family" when he "felt the crash of the explosion" as *Maine* blew up (1-24 and 1-25).

As Sigsbee groped his way in the blackness toward the outer entrance to the passageway that led to the superstructure, he collided with Pvt. William Anthony, U.S. Marine Corps (USMC) (1-26), the orderly who had been standing by the cabin door at the time of the blast and who had entered to report what had happened. Anthony apologized and declared "that the ship had blown up and was sinking."

Sigsbee soon found that there was little to be done beyond rescuing the wounded and aban-

1-24 Contemporary view of *Maine*'s destruction. Less garish than most, this view shows clearly her proximity to other ships.

1-25 Wreckage of *Maine* following the explosion of her magazines on the night of February 15, 1898.

1-26 Pvt. William Anthony, USMC

doning the doomed vessel. Almost immediately, boats from the nearby passenger liner *City of Washington* and Spanish cruiser *Alfonso XII* converged on the stricken warship to assist *Maine's* gig and whaleboat in the desperate and gruesome task. Sigsbee, the last man off the wrecked battleship, proceeded in his gig to the *City of Washington*.

Almost immediately, *Maine* became a virtual shrine. Her flag was displayed at half mast, and grieving shipmates hung wreaths from her mainmast (1-27 and 1-28). The wreck in Havana's harbor on February 16 served as an all-too-vivid reminder of the tragedy that had befallen the ship (1-29). Of

the 355 men on board, only 102 (7 of whom later succumbed to their injuries) survived. Almost 75 percent of those on board had been lost.

Spanish sailors had hastened to rescue the surviving Americans struggling in the water and Spanish doctors treated the American wounded as conscientiously as they would have their own. As the funeral procession for the victims wended its way through Havana (1-30), however, witnesses noted a marked lack of genuine sympathy on the part of the Spanish population. This perhaps could have been expected. Despite its being advertised as a goodwill mission, under the prevailing circumstances the presence in Havana

1-28 Numerous wreaths adorn *Maine's* mainmast, from which also flies the Stars and Stripes at half-mast.

1-27 American sailors close aboard *Maine* after hanging a wreath from the wrecked battleship's mainmast

1-29 *Maine's* wreck the morning after the explosion

1-30 Funeral procession for *Maine*'s dead

TWO TYPES OF CITIZENSHIP.
THE MAN WHO TALKS AND THE MAN WHO FIGHTS.

1-31 A contemporary cartoon reflects typical reactions to *Maine*'s sinking.

harbor of a United States battleship had been bound to strike the Spanish as at best an intrusion and at worst a threat.

When Sigsbee cabled the news of *Maine*'s loss to the secretary of the navy, he cautioned, "Public opinion should be suspended until further report." This was the counsel of perfection. The story was manna from Heaven for the yellow press, which devoted entire front pages to details without allowing facts to interfere with their invective. This could be the incident that pushed the country into the war that William Randolph Hearst and his ilk craved. They did not hesitate to proclaim Spanish guilt. Only a short time before, had not Enrique Dupuy de Lôme, Madrid's chief envoy to Washington, in an indiscreet letter published in Hearst's *Journal*, called President McKinley "weak and a bidder for the admiration of the crowd"?

The American public was not far behind the press (1-31). Despite the fact that the Spanish deliberately sinking an American warship would have been an act of monumental stupidity, John Q. Public had heard so much about the iniquities of the Spanish in Cuba that it was easy to cast the Spanish in the role of villain. The naval court of inquiry (1-32) concluded on March 28, 1898, "that the ship was destroyed by the explosion of a submarine mine, which caused the partial explosion of two or more of her forward magazines" but found "no evidence . . . obtainable fixing the

1-32 The *Maine* court of inquiry examines Ens. Wilfred V. N. Powelson (third from right) on board the lighthouse tender *Mangrove* in Havana harbor. Members of the court include (left to right) Capts. French E. Chadwick and William T. Sampson and Lt. Cmdrs. William R. Potter and Adolph Marix. Powelson, assigned to the transport *Fern*, headed the diving operations on *Maine*'s wreck. The court examined him on at least five occasions.

responsibility for the destruction . . . upon any person or persons." This remained the verdict for many years. Most recent research, however, leans toward the theory that spontaneous combustion in a bituminous coal bunker triggered the detonation of *Maine*'s forward magazines; the employment of a "submarine mine," by a party whose interests could have been served by such an act, cannot be lightly dismissed.

With remarkable unanimity, the U.S. Congress, the press, and the public urged McKinley to declare war and "Remember the *Maine*." Of course, more than one incident determined the course of events. A mixture of romanticism, idealism, and the country's concept of its Manifest Destiny also fueled the drive toward war (1-33). There was considerable sentiment for annexing Cuba to the United States. In Cuba, too, a number of upper- and middle-class citizens favored annexation, fearing that Cuba was ill prepared to carry on as an independent nation (1-34).

The momentum toward hostilities surged on and finally, on April 11, McKinley bowed to the seemingly inevitable and asked Congress for authority to use "the military and naval forces of the United States" against the Spanish in Cuba. After several days of wrangling, on April 14 Congress passed a resolution recognizing Cuban independence, which McKinley signed on April 20. He also signed an ultimatum, giving Spain until noon on April 23 to free Cuba (1-35). Prime Minister Práxedes Mateo Sagasta rejected the demand and severed diplomatic relations. All concerned had reached the point of no return.

1-33 *"Cuba libre!"*

1-34 The San Carlos Club in Santiago—hotbed of sentiment for the annexation of Cuba to the United States

1-35 Artist's rendition of President McKinley signing the American ultimatum to the Spanish government

CHAPTER 2

America Prepares for War

Now that the situation had moved out of the polite and proper realm of diplomacy and the shrill cries of newsprint into the chillier climes of declared war, the United States faced the problems of raising, training, and equipping a viable fighting force and transporting it to a foreign shore. This was no simple matter of rounding up the regulars and sending them to the front. In 1898 the entire U.S. Army, from commanding general to raw recruit, could have been seated comfortably in a moderate-sized college stadium. It totaled 28,000 officers and men; of these, enlisted men were limited by law to 25,000. To increase the force to 100,000, which all concerned agreed was the minimum necessary, would require an act of Congress. War having been declared, this would seem to be routine.

Congress, however, balked. To some members the request seemed a sinister scheme to saddle the American people with that bugaboo of U.S. politics—a large standing army. What really stirred up controversy, though, was the opposition of the National Guard. Many members of the local militia could be expected to enlist, and if they did so in sufficient numbers it would seriously weaken the Guard. Each governor headed his state's militia, and his right to appoint officers was a jealously guarded prerogative. In the face of necessity, however, Congress and the War Department soon worked out a compromise: the U.S. Army could reach and retain a maximum of 65,000 for two years. In the states, volunteers would be signed up on a regimental basis, with their own officers.

There was no need for "recruiting drives." War fever ran high. The war cry "Remember the *Maine*! To hell with Spain!" added a ringing phrase to whatever motivation the recruit might have. Men came forward in droves. The U.S. Army probably could have signed up ten times the authorized 65,000.

Photographs 2-1 through 2-6 show the procedure for enlisting. First came the decision to step into the recruiting office (2-1). Would he be accepted (2-2)? He must be between the ages of eighteen and thirty-five years, of good character, free of disease, and able to speak English. He must be either a citizen of the United States or have de-

2-1 A dapper prospective recruit studies enlistment circulars in front of a post office branch in New York City under the watchful eyes of a private and corporal.

2-2 Other prospects ask another corporal about enlistment.

clared his intention of becoming one. If married, he would require the approval of the regimental commander before he was accepted.

Having reviewed the qualifications and found that he met them, the recruit proceeded indoors to the squad room (2-3). If a number of men had preceded him, he would have a long wait; otherwise, he would be processed fairly rapidly. One stage of the procedure was a physical examination, and, with many more would-be soldiers than the army needed, it could afford to be choosy. Many strong and fit young men were turned

down because of varicose veins, poor teeth, or feet that tended to blister.

Safely past the physical, the candidate filled in his enlistment papers (2-4). If his data were satisfactory, he took the oath of enlistment (2-5) and was duly in the army, as sign and seal whereof he and his fellow recruits received their uniforms (2-6).

An army as small as that of the United States could not support a thriving munitions industry, and it did not have an adequate logistics backup. As a result, the army proved unable to arm, train, clothe, feed, and house properly the avalanche of

2-3 While spending "a few moments" in the squad room above the post office, recruits learn their first hard lesson about life in the Army—"Hurry up and wait."

2-5 As the recruiting sergeant looks on, an officer administers the oath of enlistment to the new enlistee.

2-4 While filling out enlistment papers, recruits undergo close questioning by the recruiting sergeant.

2-6 "You're in the Army!" Newly enlisted men draw uniforms at the recruiting station.

men that signed up. An example of poor preparation was Camp Wikoff, located at Montauk, Long Island (2-7). The fighting was over before Wikoff was established in response to Maj. Gen. William R. Shafter's plea to send his convalescents, some 75 percent of his force, to the States for recuperation. Most of these men were suffering from malaria, and Shafter feared that yellow fever would follow.

One might have expected that the War Department would have foreseen the need for a large convalescent facility in a healthful spot, but this, too, was something beyond the planning of the peacetime army. The War Department authorized the move on August 3, 1898. Work began immediately, but never caught up to the need. The troops arrived to find a welter of construction and gen-

eral confusion. Conditions gradually improved, but not enough to overcome the image of inefficiency in caring for invalids.

In general, those preparing for service in Cuba trained at southern locations, so that they could become at least partly acclimated to subtropical heat. The 1st Volunteer Cavalry, soon to become famous as the "Rough Riders," trained at San Antonio, Texas (2-8). This made sense, as the original intent was to recruit into the unit men from the Southwest. Soon, however, easterners who could prove their suitability joined the group, which thus became a true cross-section of American society.

The Rough Riders were unusually fortunate in their officers (2-9). In command was Col. Leonard Wood, a doctor by training, with a degree from

2-7 View of the training camp at Montauk, New York, on the eastern tip of Long Island

2-8 Field officers of the 1st Volunteer Cavalry, or "Rough Riders," relax in front of their tent while their unit trains at the International Fairgrounds in San Antonio, Texas, during May 1898. They are (left to right) Lt. Col. Theodore Roosevelt, Col. Leonard Wood, and Maj. Alexander Brodie.

2-9 Officer's mess in the Rough Riders' camp in San Antonio, with Colonels Wood and Roosevelt seated at the head of the table.

Harvard. He became an army surgeon and also a line officer, and earned the Medal of Honor in the Apache campaign. He was a friend of Theodore Roosevelt, who insisted that Wood, not he, command the regiment he and Wood were organizing. Roosevelt himself provided the dash and color that gave the regiment its special cachet. Wood's aide, Maj. Alexander Brodie, was a West Pointer with the gift, so valuable in an officer, of winning his men's devotion. He had lived for two decades in Arizona, and combined two features that Roosevelt particularly admired—the Westerner and the real soldier.

A portion of the trainees' time was spent in drill, designed to develop proficiency in tactics and to foster a sense of unity. Photograph 2-10 shows a New York volunteer regiment in a column of companies in close order, guiding right. The company commanders are front and center of their men,

while the staff and regimental band mill about at right. The formation was one of the last vestiges of the infantry drill so familiar to the Civil War veterans of the previous generation.

Most of the volunteers carried away from camp much less pleasant memories than that of a brisk drill under a sunny sky with good companions. Conditions in most locations were deplorable. The story is told that a Western governor objected to his militia being quartered in tents, asking plaintively, "But what if it rains?" Rain it did that May, but the men had worse to endure. Food was poor to the point where some troops were poisoned. Sanitation was far below par and disease was soon rampant. Hospital and other medical facilities were tested to the utmost (2-11).

Among the volunteers were many African Americans, formed into their own units under white officers (2-12). These men racked up a fine war

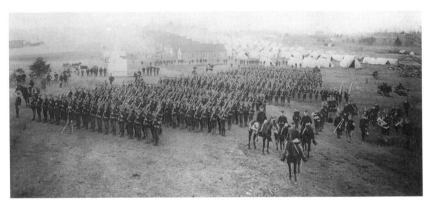

2-10 A New York volunteer infantry regiment drills in camp at Greenville, South Carolina.

2-11 Prisoners grade an area near the hospital at Camp McKenzie, Georgia.

2-12 African-American soldiers of the 3d Alabama National Guard pose at Camp Shipp, near Anniston, in east central Alabama.

record, but the Civil War was recent enough that many Southerners looked askance at black troops.

Located across the Potomac from Washington, near Fairfax, Virginia, and named for Secretary of War Russell A. Alger, Camp Alger (2-13) might have been expected to be a model facility. Instead, the reverse was true. It was large but soon filled to overflowing with ill-equipped volunteers. Such photographs as 2-13 and 2-14 give no hint of the living conditions that soon brought about a high rate of disease.

Comparatively few of the many thousands who trained at Camp Alger ever moved on to Cuba. Among them were the 8th Ohio Volunteers (2-15). Like the other volunteers, they were armed with the inadequate Springfield rifles, seen piled with other equipment in the foreground of photograph 2-16. As the 8th Ohio marched away from Camp Alger on its way to

Tampa, Florida (2-17), some may have reflected that almost forty years ago their fathers and grandfathers, too, had departed for battle in much the same fashion.

Mobilization boosted the U.S. Army's five regiments and ten battalions of artillery to seven regiments, plus volunteer batteries, to the number of eight heavy artillery and sixteen field artillery (2-18). Much was expected of these menacing-looking weapons, but during the campaign they proved a disappointment. The black-powder ammunition sent up concentrations of smoke that pinpointed the guns' positions. Moreover, the artillery officers did not seem to know how best to use their weapons, firing as individual units instead of laying down massed fire. In this respect the Americans would learn from the Spanish, who used smokeless powder and a cohesive fire pattern. But that was in the future, and for the mo-

2-13 Men line up for dinner at Camp Alger near Fairfax, Virginia.

2-14 Men at Camp Alger gather round a photographer while he works his "Biograph," preparing for a unit portrait.

2-15 Payday at Camp Alger for the 8th Ohio Volunteers, on the day they left for Tampa, Florida, in 1898

2-16 After loading a wagon, the 8th Ohio breaks camp.

2-17 The 8th Ohio marches away from Camp Alger for the last time, taking the step from regimental field music, probably the traditional tune, "The Girl I Left Behind Me."

2-18 An artillery unit's limbers lie ready for transport to Tampa, lashed and secured to the bed of a Seaboard Air Line flatcar.

2-19 The men of the 4th Artillery draw an admiring crowd as they depart for Tampa and points south.

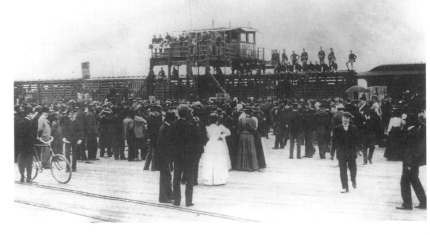

ment the artillerymen were something of the army's glamour boys (2-19).

Like the volunteers, units of the regular U.S. Army were en route to the rendezvous point at Tampa, amid the cheers of admiring well-wishers (2-20 and 2-21).

The U.S. Army had selected Tampa as the staging area because of its proximity to Cuba, its deep-water bay, and its large wharf with a rail connection into the city. At that time Tampa boasted a population of 26,000, and some 25,000 troops were training there. With virtually a one-to-one ratio, the strain on Tampa's facilities can well be imagined.

Florida was not well developed at the time, and its rail connections with other states were limited (2-22) and inadequate to handle the thousands of men and tons of material headed into the city. This was not the Florida of air-conditioned homes and luxury hotels. Most of the men carried away with them memories of scorching heat, ever-present sand, and woods and scrub that housed an active population of insects (2-23).

The only sizable structure in the city was the Tampa Bay Hotel, which had been built in a style vaguely reminiscent of North African architecture. As it was the only building in Tampa even remotely suitable, it became headquarters for the military, quartering officers and over a hundred reporters. Some of the officers' family members visited the camp (2-24) and stayed at the hotel. The hotel had a huge porch full of rocking chairs, which became a social center as officers, some of whom had not seen each other for years, gathered to reminisce and to fret at the delay in sailing for Cuba.

Roosevelt's wife, Edith, came to the Tampa Bay for a stay. Colonel Wood permitted Roosevelt to visit her, provided he returned to camp in time for reveille at 4:00 A.M., which gives some idea of the length of day the soldiers were putting in, drilling (2-25) and practicing their marksmanship (2-26). A frequent feature of camp life was

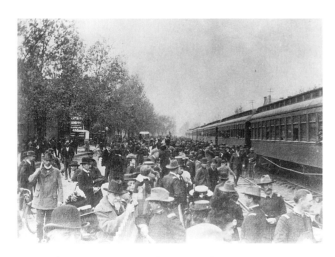

2-20 The 21st U.S. Regulars board a passenger train in Plattsburg, New York.

2-21 In a scene that must have quickened pulses and moistened many an eye, the 9th Massachusetts Volunteers depart Clinton, Massachusetts, on May 4, 1898.

2-22 Freight cars carrying equipment for the expedition to Cuba crowd into the railyard in Tampa.

2-23 The 9th U.S. Infantry, one of the most photographed units of the Santiago Campaign, encamped in a dry, sandy, piney wood in the marshaling area near Tampa.

2-24 One of the more fortunate officers, accompanied by his wife

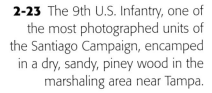

2-25 "To the rear in open order, march! Inspection arms." Troops of the 9th Infantry stand at attention for firearms inspection by a junior officer. Photographs 2-25, 2-26, and 2-27 were taken by Capt. Willis Wittich, a prolific photographer in Florida and in Cuba.

2-26 Prone firing exercises in the camps at Tampa

2-27 The 21st Infantry on a dusty practice march

the practice march, a real ordeal for men wearing heavy uniforms, laden with various impedimenta, under the searing Florida sun (2-27). They had the cold comfort of reflecting that, however bad it was in Florida, it probably would be worse in Cuba.

Maddening delays slowed the receipt of everything the troops needed, including food (2-28).

Photographs 2-29 and 2-30 show the men at mess call. Like all soldiers in all times and climes, no doubt they complained about the food.

At this time, however, they had a more pressing grievance—the delay in setting out for Cuba—because these men were genuinely eager to join battle and believed fervently in the justice of their cause.

2-28 Weighing an issue of beef for the men of the 21st Infantry.

2-29 Parched and sweat-drenched in the near-tropical Florida climate, men line up at the sound of mess call, awaiting their repast among the pines.

2-30 Regulars of Company A, 2d Infantry, mug for the camera while savoring their evening meal in Tampa.

The Antagonists

It is possible that war with Spain would have broken out much sooner than it did had William McKinley, Jr. (3-1), not been president of the United States. A substantial and ever-growing group of fire-eaters in the United States pressured for direct action to force the Spanish out of Cuba, where their methods of governing the Cubans had provoked the latter into a long conflict in an attempt to gain independence. Many Americans seem to have believed that any war was a praiseworthy expression of national virility, especially in a good cause.

McKinley, however, had served in the Civil War, where his bravery and skill had earned him a commission. He had seen war at first hand and did not like what he saw. While many politicians before and after him extolled personal virtues, McKinley quietly lived them. He neither smoked, swore, drank, played cards, nor attended the theater. Unlike some ascetics, he was genuinely kind-hearted and wished his fellow man well. It is one of history's ironies that slightly more than a year after his inauguration on March 4, 1897, he became a war president.

Leading the pack clamoring for war was the so-called yellow press, best exemplified by the New York *Journal*, published by William Randolph Hearst (3-2). The objective of Hearst and other such publishers was purely and simply to sell newspapers, and how better to do that than to feed the public with daily doses of sensational stories featuring the iniquities of the Spanish and the suf-

3-1 William McKinley, Jr., president of the United States

3-2 William Randolph Hearst, publisher of the New York *Journal*

fering of the Cubans. Some stories were exaggerated, some fabricated, but they contained enough truth to carry conviction. It did not worry Hearst and his ilk that their tactics were pushing public opinion to demand war. Purportedly, Hearst had sent the noted artist Frederic Remington to Cuba to make sketches. Finding all quiet, in January 1897 Remington advised Hearst that there was no war. "You furnish the pictures," Hearst was said to have replied, "and I'll furnish the war."

Under such circumstances, the United States minister to Spain, Stewart L. Woodford (3-3), had the unenviable task of trying to make clear the United States's firm position on Cuba and still maintain courteous diplomatic relations.

McKinley's first secretary of state was John Sherman, younger brother of Civil War General William Tecumseh Sherman. McKinley, who was a shrewd politician, elevated Sherman from the Senate to make a seat for his friend and supporter Mark A. Hanna. Sherman sympathized with the Cuban cause, but as war came ever closer, he pleaded for negotiations. McKinley turned more and more to Sherman's assistant secretary, William R. Day (3-4), and on April 25, 1898, when Sherman resigned, the president promoted Day to the secretaryship.

Russell A. Alger (3-5) brought a distinguished background to the position of secretary of war. A self-made man and a lawyer, he had fought well in the Civil War, rising to the rank of major general. In peacetime he became wealthy. He served as national commander of the Grand Army of the Republic and as governor of Michigan. However, as civilian head of the U.S. Army he was out of his depth. When Congress passed a bill authorizing $50 million to improve the armed forces, Alger took the position that only defensive measures were authorized. He seems to have had a rather naive concept of the logistics and time necessary to raise and move a large force. He and Maj. Gen. Nelson A. Miles, commanding general of the U.S. Army, quarreled to the point where McKinley turned increasingly to his capable adjutant general, Brig. Gen. Henry C. Corbin, to get things done. During the conflict the press savaged Alger mercilessly, more than his actions deserved.

The fourth estate seemed more approving of Alger's opposite, Secretary of the Navy John D. Long (3-6). Born in Maine, Long settled in Massachusetts, eventually serving in the state legislature, as lieutenant governor, and as governor before his constituents sent him to Congress. There he caught McKinley's eye and became

3-3 Stewart L. Woodford, U.S. minister to Spain

3-4 William R. Day, U.S. secretary of state

3-5 Russell A. Alger, U.S. secretary of war

secretary of the navy in 1891. Long brought to his task excellent qualifications as an administrator and as a man of character. What he lacked in technical knowledge of naval matters was balanced by the knowledge of his enthusiastic assistant secretary, Theodore Roosevelt, who loved ships and possessed a detailed knowledge of their capabilities. His *The Naval War of 1812* was already a classic. Occasionally, Roosevelt became impatient with Long's conservatism, and, while Long admired Roosevelt, he was acutely conscious of the need to rein in his assistant's belligerence. On the whole it was a productive team, however, and served the president and the country well.

The two ranking officers of the U.S. Army were Maj. Gen. Miles and Maj. Gen. William R. Shafter, who commanded V Corps (3-7). At the time of the first Battle of Bull Run, Miles had been twenty-two years old—too young, the authorities decided, to be a captain in the company of volunteers he had raised at his own expense. So he went to war as a lieutenant. In three years, after numerous battles and being twice wounded, he was a brigadier general in command of a corps. He blotted his hitherto exemplary record, however, when, as commandant at Fort Monroe, Virginia, he kept former Confederate president Jefferson Davis in chains, an unnecessary act that was resented almost as keenly in the North as in the South. He transferred to the regular army and had a successful second career against the Indians. In 1892 he belatedly received the Medal of Honor and in 1895 became commander in chief.

Like Miles, Shafter had organized and become a first lieutenant in a Civil War volunteer company, serving with distinction. Again like Miles, after the war he joined the regular army as a lieutenant colonel—in his case, of the 41st Infantry. He became a brigadier general in 1897. It is said that he was both respected and loved by the men he commanded. In May 1898, McKinley appointed him a major general in command of V Corps, consisting of 16,887 officers and men—well over half of the regular U.S. Army, plus volunteer units such as the Rough Riders. In one respect, though, Shafter seemed singularly ill-qualified for duty as a frontline general, for he weighed three hundred pounds and suffered from gout.

The declared objective of the war being to free Cuba, it was anticipated that the Cuban insurrectionist troops would be allies. The most famous leader of the Cuban forces was General Calixto García Íñiguez (3-8), commanding some five

3-6 John D. Long, U.S. secretary of the navy

3-7 Maj. Gen. William R. Shafter, commanding general, V Corps

3-8 Calixto García Íñiguez, commanding general, Cuban troops, province of Santiago

thousand troops in the province of Santiago. García would provide Shafter with much-needed intelligence about the Spanish and information concerning the terrain, and his men would participate in the battle of El Caney. Unfortunately, García's ill-clad, undisciplined men did not fit the American concept of what an army looked like and how it should behave. It was probably this nonconformity that alienated Shafter and the other American leaders. Consistent downplaying of the Cuban role, culminating in Shafter's refusal to let García's forces participate in the surrender of Santiago, deeply offended the Cuban general. Later, however, he simmered down sufficiently to visit McKinley in Washington, where he died on December 11, 1898.

No flag officer of the Spanish-American War captured the public fancy as did Commodore*

George Dewey, commander of the Asiatic Station and of the squadron in Philippine waters (3-9). The story goes that as a schoolboy, Dewey was the ringleader of a gang that had made miserable the lives of a succession of schoolmasters and gave his school the reputation of being ungovernable. He met his match in a young teacher who thrashed him severely and marched him home to receive his father's grim assurance that George would give no more trouble. He never did. He was grateful to the schoolmaster who had set him straight and who helped him prepare for the Naval Academy. Dewey served throughout the Civil War and later held a variety of positions on ship

*Commodore, a flag officer rank between captain and rear admiral, is no longer in use as such in the U.S. Navy. Dewey became a rear admiral after the Battle of Manila Bay.

3-9 Commodore George Dewey, commander, U.S. naval forces, Asiatic Station.

and ashore. He became friends with Theodore Roosevelt, who was enthusiastic about Dewey's initiative and arranged for his appointment to the command of the Asiatic Squadron.

Rear Admiral William T. Sampson, commander of the North Atlantic Station and as such in command of the naval operations off Cuba, possessed none of Dewey's charisma. He was not popular, being considered overly serious and stern. From the day in 1861 when he graduated at the head of his Naval Academy class, however, he was dedicated, intelligent, and innovative. He saw little action in the Civil War, but that little was quite enough—his ship, the monitor *Patapsco*,* fouled a mine during clearance operations in Charleston

*A monitor was a steam-powered, low-lying vessel with one or more turrets. These ships were used for coastal defense.

harbor, South Carolina, in January 1865. His subsequent career alternated sea service with increasingly important shore assignments such as superintendent of the Naval Academy, commander of the naval torpedo station at Newport, Rhode Island, and chief of the Bureau of Ordnance. Under his tenure important improvements in gunnery took place, including the introduction of smokeless powder. After the destruction of *Maine*, Sampson, then in command of the battleship *Iowa*, was named president of the naval board of inquiry. In March 1898 he was made an acting rear admiral and was given command of the North Atlantic Squadron.

In the series of events leading up to the Spanish-American War, and in the prosecution of the war itself, the future king of Spain, Alfonso XIII (3-10), played only a symbolic role. He was born on May

3-10 Alfonso XIII, king of Spain

17, 1886, the posthumous son of Alfonso XII and his second wife, the former Hapsburg archduchess María Cristina. He was only twelve years old when war broke out and had not yet assumed the throne. The little fellow was not robust, but he was in good hands. As queen regent, María Cristina (3-11), an intelligent woman of noble character, was devoted to the interests of her adopted country and especially to those of her son.

A constant threat to the succession was the pretender, Don Carlos (3-12). Indeed, some years before, he had been offered the throne on condition that he support the proposed liberal constitution and separation of church and state. "When I come to my throne," he had replied haughtily, "I shall rule my land as I see fit." This had killed his chances with the more liberal elements, but many Spaniards considered him the legitimate king of

Spain and worked enthusiastically in his cause. Not a particularly admirable character, he had the knack of inspiring devotion, and an uprising in his favor, if no more than a nuisance, was always a possibility.

Another potential source of trouble was General Valeriano Weyler y Nicolau (3-13), the notorious "Butcher" Weyler, of German extraction. His rise in the Spanish army was rapid. Among other duties, he was the military attaché in Washington during the Civil War. Then he was sent to Cuba at the head of a division. He became a general in 1888 and eight years later was appointed governor general of Cuba, which was in revolt again. An arrogant man who despised the Cubans, he had an overwhelming superiority in manpower—more than 200,000 men as opposed to never more than 30,000 insurgents. Faced with guerrilla

3-12 Don Carlos, pretender to the Spanish throne

3-11 María Cristina of Austria, queen regent and mother of Alfonso XIII

warfare against which conventional tactics proved practically worthless, he instituted a process of destroying the rebels' base of support, moving more than 300,000 rural Cubans into so-called reconcentration camps; hence, these unfortunates were known as *reconcentrados*. No provision was made for food, sanitation, or health care, and thousands died miserably. The Cubans and the Americans were horrified; a storm of protest blew across the pages of the U.S. press.

Weyler was recalled to Spain late in 1897. This was principally due to political events in Spain, where his main supporter, Prime Minister Antonio Cánovas del Castillo, had been assassinated, but many Spaniards saw in his return a surrender to American protests. This did not sit well in some quarters, and there was talk of a possible coup to make Weyler dictator of Spain.

Cánovas's successor was Práxedes Mateo Sagasta (3-14). His family was not wealthy, and he was an engineer by profession. Soon he became involved in the reform movement in Spanish politics. He founded the Liberal Party and led the revolution that dethroned Queen Isabella II, an individual in notable contrast to the distinguished first Isabella. In the ups and downs of Spanish politics he was prime minister no less than five times, the last appointment coming with the assassination of Cánovas on August 8, 1897. He tried to ease the situation in Cuba, recalling Weyler and offering autonomy to Cuba and Puerto Rico, but by this time the Cubans wanted nothing short of independence. He abandoned politics after the end of the Spanish-American War in the face of severe criticism for making peace with the United States.

3-13 General Valeriano Weyler y Nicolau, governor general of Cuba before the outbreak of hostilities

3-14 Práxedes Mateo Sagasta, Spanish prime minister

Sagasta's minister of war, Miguel Correa, was a veteran of some fifty years in the Spanish army. Naturally enough, he had considerable confidence that the army could hold the line, but he was pessimistic about the chances of Spain's navy. He kept in close touch by cable with the governor general of the Philippines, Basilio Augustín Dávila, and Cuba's new governor general, Capt. Gen. Ramón Blanco y Erenas (3-15).

Blanco had served in the same position in the Philippines. In accordance with Sagasta's policies and his own inclination, Blanco performed his duties with much less severity than had Weyler. He released a number of political prisoners and appointed only creoles—individuals born in Cuba of Spanish parentage—to his new governing council. This angered the *peninsulares*, immigrants from Spain, who considered themselves superior to the creoles and who had hitherto dominated the Cuban government and economy. Blanco meant well, but the situation was beyond compromise. The insurgents demanded independence, not autonomy, and the loyalists wanted a return to the "good old days" of Weyler. Rioting broke out in Havana in January 1898, prompting

U.S. consul Fitzhugh Lee to question Blanco's ability to maintain order. Lee's request for American warships to protect U.S. lives and property—another step on the road to war—led to *Maine* being dispatched to the scene.

Most of the land action in Cuba would be fought in the area of Santiago, where Brig. Gen. Arsenio Linares y Pomba was in command of the army corps defending it (3-16). All Spanish troops, numbering 28,218 officers and men, were under his command, but well over half were distributed across the whole district, so that by June 20 his force at Santiago itself was about 9,400. Linares had served in Cuba before, as well as in the Philippines and against the Carlists in Spain. A good soldier, he would personally lead his men in the fighting around San Juan Hill, where he would be severely wounded and have to be evacuated to the rear.

At that time, commanding the Spanish squadron at Santiago against his will was Admiral Pascual Cervera y Topete (3-17). The minister of marine, Admiral Segismundo Bermejo y Merelo, had an inflated notion of Spain's naval capabilities. Among other illusions, he expected Cervera,

3-15 Capt. Gen. Ramón Blanco y Erenas, governor general of Cuba

3-16 Brig. Gen. Arsenio Linares y Pomba, commanding general, army corps, Santiago

then in command of the squadron at Cádiz, to level Key West and harass the U.S. eastern coastal cities in the event of war with the United States. Cervera, who had been naval attaché at Washington and spoke excellent English, realistically knew that his forces were no match for the Americans and considered Cuba lost from the moment war was declared. He believed the best he could do was defend the Spanish coast and the Canary Islands against U.S. naval raiders. Bermejo, however, ordered the fleet to the Caribbean. To make matters worse, the new minister of marine, Capt. Rámon Auñón y Villalón, placed Cervera under Blanco's command after he reached Cuban waters, which further hindered Cervera's freedom of action. The Americans came to respect Cervera for his good sense, chivalry toward his opponents, and stoicism in disaster.

Dewey's victory at Manila Bay shocked Spain and presented Auñón with a dilemma. He must attempt to hold the Philippines, but if he sent the fleet currently in home waters under Admiral Manuel de la Cámara y Libermoore (3-18) to the rescue, Spain's home ports would be unprotected. He decided to take the risk and dispatched Cámara's fleet on June 16. American officials, unsure that Dewey could overcome this new threat, sent him the monitors *Monterey* and *Monadnock*. They were not needed; Cámara's ships never made it past the Suez Canal. The British authorities at Port Said refused to coal the Spanish ships, and on July 7 Auñón ordered Cámara to return.

Spain's naval forces at Manila were under the command of Admiral Patricio Montojo y Parasón (3-19), an experienced officer who wrote novels in his spare time. His fleet numbered thirty-seven,

3-18 Admiral Manuel de la Cámara y Libermoore, commander, Spanish naval squadron in Spanish waters

3-17 Admiral Pascual Cervera y Topete, commander, Spanish naval squadron before Santiago

but most were little more than armed launches. He had only seven ships that could be considered fit for combat. He might have fought a delaying action by spreading his ships through the islands, but political considerations made it impossible for him to leave Manila unprotected. So his fleet fell victim to Dewey. After the war, Montojo was court-martialed and convicted of dereliction of duty, but because no one could deny that he and his men had fought gallantly, his sentence was only dismissal from the navy—a bitter enough punishment.

As these individuals, the good and the not so good, the daring and the cautious, took their places on the short-lived but fascinating chess-board of the Spanish-American War, a number of illusions existed. Perhaps it was difficult to accept that Spain, with its centuries of warrior tradition, no longer wielded a significant military and naval power. A number of Americans living in East Coast cities feared that Spanish warships, reputed to be faster than American ships, would speed across the Atlantic and shell their homes. On the other hand, many Europeans, not all of them Spaniards, had a low opinion of the U.S. Navy. Its crews were supposed to be composed of mercenaries, the refuse of European ports, who would desert in droves at the first shot.

There was much to be learned, not only about men, but also about their arms and equipment.

3-19 Admiral Patricio Montojo y Parasón, commander, Spanish naval squadron off Manila Bay

CHAPTER 4

The Tools of War

A group picture of U.S. Army regulars taken at the onset of the Spanish-American War (4-1) could have been mistaken for a similar group of American soldiers during the Civil War. The Union men would have been immediately familiar with the slouch hat, blanket roll, haversack, canteen, and tin cup with which the new men were burdened. And they would have recognized the traditional army blues and experienced a pang of pity for their successors. These uniforms were of heavy wool and would have been comfortable in Alaska. As clothing to be worn in Cuba in the summer, they were little short of torture. Some of the volunteers fared better in that respect. The Rough Riders, for example, had khaki uniforms, and the Marines had brown linen campaign uniforms by the time they sailed for Cuba.

If the personal equipment looked to the past, battlefield tactics looked to the future. The massed infantry movements of which Napoleon had been a master were no longer practicable. So the trainees at Tampa were instructed in spread-out formations and were encouraged to dig in at every turn (4-2). The day of the foxhole had arrived.

While personal equipment had been relatively unchanged for thirty years and tactics were in transition, in weaponry the U.S. Army had made a quantum leap forward. America's first modern rifle and cavalry carbine, the Krag-Jörgensen Model 1892 .30 caliber (4-3), was introduced in 1894 after exhaustive tests. The Krag was far more effective than the previous .45-.70 single-shot Springfields. It featured a bolt action and five-shot magazine, feeding from right to left and thence upward into the chamber. Its ammunition employed smokeless powder and thus hastened the transition in war to the "invisible enemy." The Krag's primary drawback was that it required five

4-1 U.S. regulars from the 12th Infantry stand ready for action, armed with Krag-Jörgensen rifles.

4-2 American infantry dug in on a firing line during exercises in camp near Tampa.

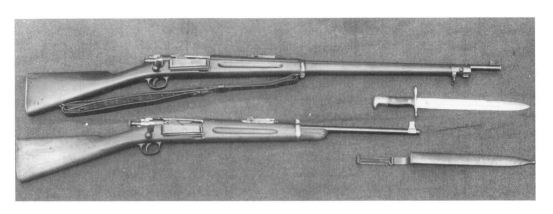

4-3 Krag-Jörgensen Model 1892 .30-caliber rifle and cavalry carbine, both generally issued to regulars. Note the snap-on, tinned hood covering the carbine's front sight, in place to protect the sight in the saddle scabbard.

individual cartridges to be loaded into a cumbersome, folding side magazine. A web belt issued to the regulars held two double rows of cartridges, totaling 100 rounds, and also featured a first-aid kit suspended from the bottom of the belt.

Unfortunately, there were only enough Krag-Jörgensens available to supply the regulars. Volunteer units had to settle for the Springfield Model 1873 .45-.70-caliber rifle (4-4). An exception was the 1st U.S. Volunteer Cavalry, better known as the Rough Riders, of which Theodore Roosevelt was lieutenant colonel. He was not the man to settle for second best, and he used his political clout to arm his men with Krags.

Almost an artifact of the Civil War, the .45-.70 was not far removed from its .58-caliber muzzle-loading predecessor. In order to be more efficient, .45-caliber ammunition was initiated. This represented the first reduction in caliber applied to regular army rifles. While its distinctive "trapdoor" (used first in the 1870 .50-caliber model) allowed for breech-loading convenience, the rate of fire was far below that of the bolt-action Spanish Mausers. Like the Krag, the Springfield had a range of two miles, and it had a stronger impact. But its cartridges still used black powder (smokeless cartridges were in short supply), which pinpointed the location of the user. Most volunteer units in Cuba were equipped with this weapon. The still relatively large caliber of the Springfield meant that its web cartridge belts held only 50 rounds, as opposed to the 100-cartridge Krag belts.

Although artillery pieces in use in 1898 were much improved over their Civil War counterparts, U.S. tactics were much the same as in previous decades. The automotive age was not far in the future, but at this time movement of artillery still depended on literal horsepower (4-5).

A relatively new weapon that had seen limited service in the Civil War was the Gatling gun (4-6). About 150 of these close-support machine guns with rotating barrels were available in 1898, fifteen of which were earmarked for Cuba. Capt. John N. Parker organized a detachment armed with these weapons to serve under Shafter, and they played a significant role in the battle of El Caney. Firing 500 shots a minute, the Gatling gun had a shattering effect on enemy morale.

A trademark for the Rough Riders and the men of Maj. Gen. "Fighting Joe" Wheeler's cavalry division was the Sims-Dudley dynamite gun (4-7). This weapon was actually an oversized air rifle, firing a dynamite-filled cartridge propelled by compressed air generated by the discharge of a blank cartridge in the lower barrel. The dynamite gun was the center of much press attention during the siege of Santiago. The gun pictured in photograph 4-7 was displayed in the New York City military shop of the renowned dealer in military surplus, Francis Bannerman, as late as the 1920s.

Transport of supplies overland was still the province of the lowly, and sometimes recalcitrant, army pack mule (4-8). As indispensable as it was exasperating, the army mule is still honored as the mascot of the U.S. Military Academy. The mule-powered ambulance shown in photograph 4-9 was little changed from the Civil War period. The efficiency of overland movement depended to a large extent on the state of the road system. U.S. soldiers en route to Cuba may have envisioned a network

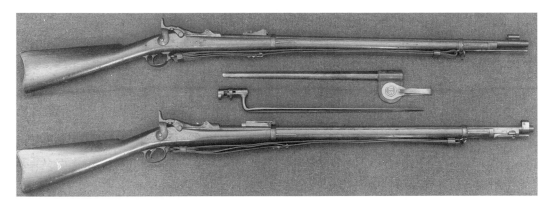

4-4 Springfield rifles, Model 1873, .45-.70 caliber, issued to volunteer units due to a shortage of Krag-Jörgensens

4-5 A horse-drawn artillery piece with limber in one of the many camps surrounding Tampa during the summer of 1898

4-6 A Gatling gun parked in the tall grass behind the siege lines at Santiago

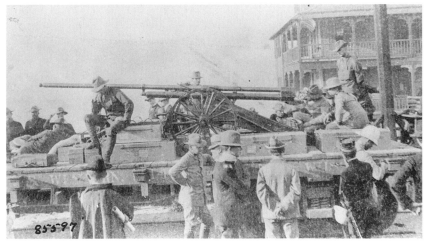

4-7 The famous Sims-Dudley dynamite gun in Tampa on its way to a Cuba-bound transport, probably *Leona*, to which the 10th Cavalry was assigned

4-8 Army pack mules during the Santiago Campaign

4-9 A mule-drawn U.S. Army ambulance before being loaded at Tampa

of roads similar to the spacious, tidy thoroughfare pictured in photograph 4-10. The reality, however, was more often closer to "unimproved hogpaths," hardly more than openings through the brush (4-11). The impenetrable, inhospitable countryside itself was used tactically by both sides.

Much of the action in the Spanish-American War was naval. At the center of that action in Cuban waters were four coast battleships. Three—*Indiana*, *Massachusetts*, and *Oregon* (4-12)—were of the *Indiana* class. Each had a main battery of four 13-inch/.35-caliber breech-loading rifles (BLRs) in two turrets and a secondary battery of eight 8-inch/.35-caliber BLRs and four 6-inch/.40-caliber BLRs. This class displaced 10,288 tons and had a maximum speed of 15.5 knots. Their range was limited by their small coal capacity. They were low-slung and frequently shipped water, which hampered firing.

Oregon, the newest of the three, was commissioned on July 15, 1896. The newest coast battleship was *Iowa*, commissioned on June 16, 1897. *Iowa*'s main battery consisted of four 12-inch/.35-caliber BLRs. Although built close in time to the *Indiana* class, *Iowa* marked an improvement in shipbuilding, displacing 11,340 tons and capable of a 17-knot speed. These four vessels were easily the most powerful in the U.S. Navy in 1898.

Photograph 4-13 shows crewmen loading an 8-inch/.35-caliber BLR on board *New York*. This type of gun was the main battery in the armored cruisers *New York* and *Brooklyn* and the secondary battery of battleships of the *Indiana* class. Very fast and with an improved propulsion system, *New York* became the flagship of the North Atlantic Squadron.

Amazonas was built in England, originally for Brazil, but before her completion the United

4-10 The main road leading to Güines, Cuba

4-11 The "road" between La Sierra and San Blas, Cuba

4-12 The battleship *Oregon* off San Francisco, March 19, 1898

States purchased her from the Brazilian government. Her official name change to *New Orleans* did not catch up with the ship until her arrival in the United States. Photograph 4-14 shows her mooring astern of the receiving ship *Vermont* after her voyage from England, manned by a crew drawn from the complement of the armored cruiser *San Francisco*.

A number of ships serving in the Spanish-American War on both sides were converted from civilian status. One such was the auxiliary cruiser *Yankee* (4-15), which originally was the *El Norte*, a Morgan Line passenger steamer. She proved to be a useful addition to the fleet.

The same could not be said of the monitors (4-16) called into service. Almost constantly awash and rolling, too slow to keep up with the other ships, and vulnerable to torpedo boat attack, monitors had long since outlived their usefulness. But a few were put into service, principally to calm jittery citizens of the U.S. coastal regions who feared Spanish raids.

A sharp disillusionment awaited U.S. soldiers when they reached Cuba. Fed by stories from the press and tabloids, Americans harbored somewhat naive notions regarding the "gallant Cubans" (4-17). They were disappointed and disconcerted by the backward nature of the Cuban peasants and by the cruelty the Cuban insurgents exhibited.

Photograph 4-18 represents what most Americans saw of the Cuban soldiers—a hard-fighting, ragtag multitude of irregulars. General García's troops drew supplies and clothing from any available source, but the preferred "uniform" was simply white or tan duck, with a straw hat. When an engagement went to close quarters, the insurgents tended to throw away their firearms and take to their more familiar machetes.

Although the Spanish troops pictured in photograph 4-19 were stationed in Puerto Rico, they were typical of their compatriots in Cuba—brave, hard-fighting, and a formidable foe. Unfortunately for them, all too often they were poorly and indifferently led. The Spaniards' strong suits were that they were acclimated to the harsh Cuban climate, knew the country, and were used to hard campaigning brought about by the Cuban insurgency. The main Spanish weakness lay in the defensive

4-13 Sailors practice loading one of the 8-inch/.35-caliber BLRs of the armored cruiser *New York*, circa 1898.

4-14 After her maiden voyage from England, the armored cruiser *Amazonas* (soon to be renamed *New Orleans*) arrives at the New York Navy Yard on April 15, 1898.

4-15 The auxiliary cruiser *Yankee* fits out at the New York Navy Yard on April 27, 1898.

4-16 The Civil War–era monitor, *Jason*, originally named *Sangamon* and a veteran of service in the North Atlantic and South Atlantic blockading squadrons, fits out at the New York Navy Yard on May 28, 1898.

4-17 Proud and defiant, a Cuban soldier is ready for action against the Spanish.

4-18 Cuban irregulars meet Americans during the advance from Siboney in June 1898.

4-19 Members of the 25th Company, Alfonso Guards, stand proudly in front of their barracks in Puerto Rico.

strategy of holding a large number of strong-points, most of which would never be attacked. This practice ensured that the Spanish army would always be scattered and could never mass at important points to outnumber the enemy. Had General Linares concentrated his army before Shafter's, he could easily have outnumbered his foe nearly two to one. As much difficulty as the Americans experienced in the face of the poorly handled Spanish army, it is hard to imagine that they would have been successful had Linares effected a significant concentration.

The Spanish army's morale was much affected by the Cuban monetary crisis, particularly acute near Santiago, with the paper currency being greatly depreciated. The Spanish troops at Santiago had not been paid in months, and when they finally were paid, the Spanish notes were worth only sixty-four cents on the dollar in gold. Predictably, the American blockade dried up supplies, particularly the army's rations. All told, Linares's soldiers near Santiago were in a wretched condition—ill-paid and ill-fed—not the kind of troops who could be expected to win a campaign.

The Spanish soldier carried the Mauser Model 1893 rifle (4-20), a weapon superior to the Americans' Krag-Jörgensen in muzzle velocity and penetrating power. It was far easier and quicker to load the five-round clip of smokeless 7mm cartridges into its internal box magazine, as opposed to feeding individual cartridges into the Krag. The United States had considered adopting the Mauser but decided on the Krag-Jörgensen. Fortunately for the Americans, the technical excellence of the Mauser was largely negated by the average Spanish soldier's poor marksmanship, in large part the result of a lack of target practice. Even so, Mausers inflicted more than 1,400 American casualties at San Juan Hill.

Many Spanish soldiers were quartered in Mercedes Barracks near Santiago (4-21). Americans knew these barracks as the place of imprisonment of Assistant Naval Constructor Richmond Pearson Hobson of *New York* and of the volunteers who had tried unsuccessfully to sink the

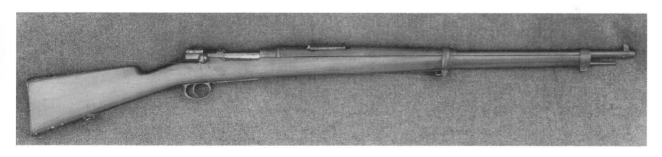

4-20 The Spanish Mauser, Model 1893, issued to Spanish troops serving in Cuba

4-21 The Mercedes Barracks, situated on a broad plateau outside the city of Santiago

collier *Merrimac* in the channel leading into Santiago harbor. The Spanish, however, treated Hobson and his men more like honored guests than prisoners.

Spanish defensive strategy featured the construction of a large number of earthen redoubts, such as those in photographs 4-22 and 4-23, to augment the sometimes centuries-old stone fortifications guarding Cuban cities and ports. The barbed wire in front of the Spanish positions such as Redoubt Mazo (4-24) was a grim harbinger of the static trench warfare that would follow during World War I.

When it was necessary to transport troops through hostile Cuban territory, the Spaniards used special armored trains (4-25). Artillery in the field and along the coast ranged from modern, rifled, breech-loading guns (4-26) to those reflecting bygone years, dating from the American Civil War (4-27) and much earlier (4-28). Photograph 4-29 shows Morro Castle looming over guns protecting Santiago harbor. The old Spanish fortifications about Santiago, Havana, and other places, were reminders of a glorious colonial and imperial tradition, now decayed and run to seed (4-30 and 4-31).

Characteristic of the Spanish strongpoint mentality (such as would capture the French imagination in Indochina) were the ubiquitous blockhouses (4-32), which were of every construction method and adaptation imaginable. The most common variety in open areas was of lumber and earthen construction, fabricated in a manner similar to the "post hole" houses of colonial America. Upper levels of the blockhouses (4-33) (and any appended structures) often were set at 45 degrees to provide eight angles of fire and were loopholed with narrow slits to provide maxi-

4-22 Redoubt Chipre outside the city of Havana, Cuba. Note the sandbagged construction.

4-23 Redoubt Mordazo, a Spanish log-and-sand earthwork in the network of defenses surrounding Havana

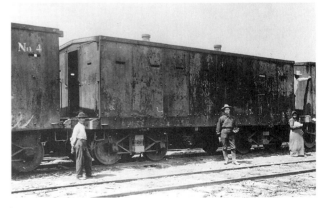

4-24 Barbed-wire entanglements in front of Redoubt Mazo near Havana

4-25 Armored railway cars at Sagua la Grande, Cuba

4-26 A 12-inch gun at the Santa Clara battery near Vedado

4-27 Large-bore muzzle-loading Parrott rifles on the Santiago defenses

4-28 Smoothbore, 5-inch Spanish artillery piece from the early nineteenth century in the defensive lines before Santiago

4-29 Hotchkiss guns guard the entrance to Santiago harbor. Morro Castle lies in the background.

4-30 Spanish fort at the harbor near Cienfuegos, Cuba

4-31 Draw-bridge and entrance to the keep of El Castillo at Cienfuegos

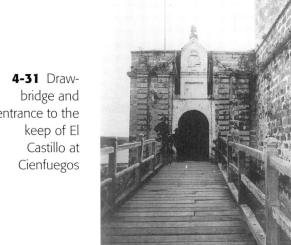

4-32 Spanish blockhouse under construction near Santiago

mum cover for those firing from inside. Usually, the blockhouses were manned by a six- to twelve-man detachment, which was almost impervious to rifle fire but was susceptible to artillery fire. Occasionally, residences were appropriated, loopholed, and converted into strongpoints at strategic locations (4-34). Even churches could not escape the Spaniard's grasp, as the incorporation of the structure shown in photograph 4-35 attests. Occasionally, the Spanish erected modern concrete structures at particularly important locations, such as a railway passing track (4-36).

Some Spanish leaders knew, while others refused to recognize, that Spain's fighting ships were not capable of trying conclusions with the U.S. Navy. The four vessels visible anchored in the left background of photograph 4-37 were probably the best available. *Almirante Oquendo*, *Infanta María Teresa*, *Vizcaya*, and *Cristóbal Colón* were armored cruisers, the first three sister ships, slightly under 7,000 tons. Barbettes for their two 11-inch guns were lightly armored, and the 5.5-inch guns (4-38) had only shields. Ammunition hoists had no cover. Too much wood had been used in their construction, rendering them fire-traps. Moreover, the Spanish captains did not hold frequent crew drills while in port, so it is doubtful that these men were ready for combat.

Cristóbal Colón had been built in Italy but before completion had been sent to Barcelona in 1898 for the finishing touches. With an armor belt, ten 6-inch Armstrong guns, and six 5-inch guns, she displaced 6,840 tons and could attain 20 knots. Theoretically, she should have been able to

4-33 Completed blockhouse at Caibarién, Cuba

4-34 Loopholed house at La Sierra

4-35 Spanish blockhouse converted from a church near Rincón

4-36 Blockhouse commanding the north end of a railroad embankment near Isabella de Saqua

hold her own against any individual American ship, but there had not been enough time to install the two 10-inch Armstrong guns called for in her design, so she had no main battery. Ammunition was in such short supply that she could not conduct target practice, and her crew did not have sufficient time to become used to her before she sailed.

It is apparent that the Spanish soldiers in Cuba—brave, climate hardened, and well armed—with competent leadership could have prolonged the war and inflicted heavy casualties. The same cannot be said of the Spanish navy. The problems lay in the ships themselves. Cervera had been fully justified in his pessimism: no matter how the land war went, the outcome would be decided at sea. A nation bent on retaining a rebellious island possession must have command of the waters around it. The Cubans had no navy, but the U.S. declaration of war tilted the balance beyond restoration.

4-37 Admiral Cervera's squadron at Saint Vincent, Cape Verde Islands, between April 19 and 29, 1898

4-38 A sailor on board the Spanish armored cruiser *Vizcaya* demonstrates the workings of 5.5-inch gun, the standard secondary battery weapon on board that vessel and her two ill-fated sister ships, *Almirante Oquendo* and *Infanta María Teresa*.

CHAPTER 5

Victory at Manila Bay

On February 25, 1898, ten days after the sinking of *Maine*, Secretary of the Navy John D. Long did a rash thing—he took a day off, leaving his assistant secretary, Theodore Roosevelt, in charge. Long left a handwritten note making it clear that, while he wanted Roosevelt to "look after the routine of the office," he wanted "no sensation in the papers."

He should have known better. Roosevelt erupted in a volcano of orders and directives, all aimed at increasing the navy's readiness for imminent war. Among them, he cabled Commodore Dewey, whose Asiatic Squadron lay at Yokohama, Japan: "Order the squadron except the *Monocacy* [an antiquated side-wheel gunboat] to Hong Kong. Keep full of coal. In the event of a declaration of war with Spain, your duty will be to see that the Spanish Squadron does not leave the Asiatic coast, and then offensive operations in the Philippine Islands. Keep *Olympia* until further notice."

When Long returned the next day, he was horrified. While he canceled some of his subordinate's directives, he did not rescind the message to Dewey. After all, Roosevelt had only done what would have to be done sooner or later.

Dewey's orders took him much closer to the potential scene of action. His force seemed far from formidable. In fact, there was only one first-class warship in the Pacific—the 10,288-ton battleship *Oregon*—and she would not be available to Dewey, because she had been reassigned to the North Atlantic Squadron with the concentration of the fleet to prepare for the main clash in the Atlantic. On March 19, 1898, *Oregon* (5-1) began the long journey from San Francisco to the Straits of Magellan and north through the South Atlantic to Florida. She arrived at Key West on May 24. Before firing a shot, *Oregon* served her country well by demonstrating the need for a canal across the Isthmus of Panama. Future wars would not wait for replacement ships to take a two-month voyage around the Horn.

Meanwhile, Dewey, on board his flagship *Olympia* (5-2) at Hong Kong, hastened to ready his squadron for the impending conflict. *Olympia's* skipper, Capt. Charles V. Gridley (5-3), although he was terminally ill and had been ordered home, insisted on remaining in command even though his replacement, Cmdr. Benjamin P. Lamberton, had arrived on the Asiatic Station. Dewey made Lamberton his chief of staff.

Knowing that when the expected declaration of war came he would have to remove his squadron from Hong Kong—neutral British territory—Dewey arranged for temporary facilities at nearby Mirs Bay in China. He also ordered his ships' peacetime white-and-straw color replaced by lead gray and acquired two merchant vessels with their cargoes. The protected cruiser *Baltimore* (5-4), en route from Honolulu via Yokohama with a supply of ammunition, reached Hong Kong

5-1 The battleship *Oregon* during its voyage around South America to Cuba

5-2 The protected cruiser *Olympia* at Hong Kong, circa April 1898. Note that lead gray color has replaced the peacetime white-and-straw scheme. Commodore George Dewey's flag flies on the main.

5-3 Capt. Charles V. Gridley, *Olympia*'s commanding officer

5-4 Postwar view of the protected cruiser *Baltimore*, in peacetime white-and-straw color scheme, with laundry festooning the forward rigging

under her commander, Capt. Nehemiah M. Dyer (5-5), on April 22. During the next two days the cruiser's bottom was scraped and she was painted, provisioned, and fueled.

It was just in time, for on April 24, 1898, the Navy Department telegraphed Dewey: "War has commenced between the United States and Spain. Proceed at once to the Philippine Islands. Com-

mence operations at once, particularly against the Spanish fleet. You must capture vessels or destroy. Use utmost endeavors."

As expected, the British gave Dewey twenty-four hours to leave Hong Kong, but he did not require that long to move to Mirs Bay, sent on his way with the good wishes, but pessimistic expectations, of his former hosts, who apparently shared

5-5 Capt. Nehemiah M. Dyer, *Baltimore*'s commanding officer

the predominant exaggerated opinion of the Spanish navy's prowess. "In the Hong Kong Club," Dewey observed later, "it was not possible to get bets, even at heavy odds, that our expedition would be a success."

Although to reporter John T. McCutcheon of the Chicago *Record*, "The combined fleet seemed to be very formidable," by the standards of twentieth-century naval warfare it looked pitiably small. Besides *Olympia* and *Baltimore*, it included the

protected cruiser *Raleigh* (5-6), a 300-foot vessel of 3,213 tons under the command of Capt. Joseph B. Coghlan (5-7). *Raleigh* carried four torpedo tubes, one 6-inch gun, ten 5-inch guns, and several others of smaller caliber. Designed for speed, *Raleigh* had unusually large engines and boilers, and the temperature below decks had been known to reach 200 degrees Fahrenheit. Needless to say, this floating oven was not popular with officers and crew.

5-6 The protected cruiser *Raleigh*

5-7 Capt. Joseph B. Coghlan, *Raleigh*'s commanding officer

Dewey's squadron included two gunboats, the 892-ton *Petrel* (5-8) under Cmdr. Edward P. Wood (5-9), and the 710-ton *Concord* (5-10) under Cmdr. Asa Walker (5-11). Carrying more clout was the protected cruiser *Boston* (5-12), one of the first steel ships of the "New Navy," a vessel of 3,189 tons armed with two 8-inch, six 6-inch, and ten smaller guns. Her commanding officer, Capt. Frank Wildes

5-8 The gunboat *Petrel* at Hong Kong, April 15, 1898

5-9 Cmdr. Edward P. Wood, *Petrel*'s commanding officer

5-10 The gunboat *Concord*

5-11 Cmdr. Asa Walker, *Concord*'s commanding officer

5-12 The protected cruiser *Boston*

5-13 Capt. Frank Wildes, *Boston*'s commanding officer

5-14 The revenue cutter *McCulloch* served as a valuable auxiliary to Dewey's squadron.

5-15 Capt. Daniel B. Hodgsdon, Revenue Cutter Service, *McCulloch*'s commanding officer

(5-13), eagerly retained his command, although he had received orders to return to the United States.

The revenue cutter *McCulloch* (5-14), under Capt. Daniel Hodgsdon (5-15), of the Revenue Cutter Service (forerunner of the modern Coast Guard), was attached to Dewey's squadron. Although not in the line of battle on May 1, she would accompany the warships as they ran the batteries at the entrance of Manila Bay. Dewey kept *McCulloch* nearby "in readiness to assist any vessel that might be disabled." Unglamorous but necessary were the auxiliary vessels that Dewey had added to his force, the supply ship *Zafiro* (5-16) and the collier *Nanshan* (5-17).

The Asiatic Squadron spent three days at Mirs Bay, busy with last-minute preparations. The ammunition that *Baltimore* had brought was distributed to the other warships, and some wooden items that could be spared were removed. On the afternoon of April 27, Dewey's little fleet stood out, shaping course for the Philippines. Shortly thereafter, the commodore had each captain assemble his crew so that he could read to them a translation of a letter composed by the archbishop of Manila and made public by the newly appointed governor general of the Philippines, Basilio Augustín Dávila:

> . . . The North American people, constituted of all social excrescences, have exhausted our patience and provoked war by their perfidious machinations, their acts of treachery, their outrages against the laws of nations and international conventions.

> Spain . . . will emerge triumphant from this new test, humiliating and blasting the adventurers from those states that, without cohesion and without history, offer to humanity only infamous tradition and . . . insolence, cowardice and cynicism.

> A squadron manned by foreigners possessing neither instruction nor discipline, is preparing to come to this archipelago with ruffianly intention, robbing us of all that means life, honor, and liberty, and pretending to be inspired by a courage of which they are incapable . . . Vain designs! Ridiculous boastings! . . .

This effusion made the day of the American sailors, who responded with laughter, catcalls, and spontaneous singing of "Yankee Doodle" and "The Star-Spangled Banner."

Luzon came into view on the morning of April 30, and the squadron spent the day preparing for the battle anticipated at dawn the next morning. Dewey expected to find the Spanish fleet at Subic Bay, some fifty miles west of Manila, and indeed that is where Admiral Montojo had planned to place his ships. When Montojo arrived, however, he found the fortifications in an appalling state. No heavy guns were in place, very few mines had been sown, and time did not permit these deficiencies to be corrected. Therefore, Montojo took his ships back to Manila Bay, prepared to fight at Cavite.

Although a brave man, Montojo was too experienced a sailor to entertain illusions, and he fully expected decisive defeat. Naval tacticians have suggested that Montojo should have dispersed his ships instead of giving battle, thus

5-16 The supply ship *Zafiro*

5-17 The collier *Nanshan*, December 26, 1915

sending Dewey on a frustrating and time-consuming hunt through the innumerable islands of the archipelago, thousands of miles from any American naval installation and perhaps giving Spain time to send reinforcements to the Philippines. Governor General Augustín, however, would not hear of any plan that did not include the defense of Manila, and Montojo, too, was not eager to leave the capital to the Americans. To spare the city possible bombardment, he moved his squadron six miles from Manila and on April 29 anchored in Cañacao Bay near the Cavite naval dockyard and under the guns of Sangley Point.

Meanwhile, Dewey reconnoitered Subic Bay and found it empty. For his part, Montojo received word on April 30 that the American squadron had been seen off Subic, headed toward Manila, but, incredibly, he and a number of his officers went to Manila to attend a reception. The kindest rationale for this extraordinary action is that possibly Montojo did not expect Dewey to dare the mine-infested waters of the Boca Grande channel until daylight.

Dewey had no intention of waiting for the sun. He summoned his captains to *Olympia* to give them his instructions, and by seven that evening

Olympia was under way. Following her at intervals of 400 yards, in total darkness except for a stern light on each ship, were the other vessels of Dewey's small force. It was a clear moonlit night, war had been declared, and the Spanish knew that the American Asiatic Squadron was in the area. By any standards Dewey could expect heavy resistance. So, at 9:15 P.M., the men were given instructions to man their guns. The squadron might have reached Manila without being spotted except for a freak accident—the soot in *McCulloch*'s funnel caught fire and burned brightly if fleetingly. There was a brief exchange of fire; then *McCulloch*'s funnel flamed again. The Spaniards on Corregidor were watching now but did not fire. Fifteen minutes after midnight, the guns on El Fraile spoke; *Boston* and *McCulloch* replied. Nothing further occurred and the Americans pressed on. The passage had not been made without cost; *McCulloch*'s chief engineer collapsed of heat prostration when the ship's funnel caught fire. He died at 2:15 A.M.

Officers and men took a coffee-and-hardtack break at 4:00 A.M. and about half an hour later dawn broke. The squadron surged forward—first *Olympia*, then *Baltimore*, *Raleigh*, *Petrel*, *Concord*, and *Boston* (5-18). At approximately 5:00 A.M., Sun-

5-18 Alfonso Saenz's depiction of the Battle of Manila Bay, showing the protected cruiser *Olympia* leading the American line of battle. The protected cruisers *Baltimore* and *Raleigh* and gunboats *Petrel* and *Concord* follow; the protected cruiser *Boston* brings up the rear.

day, May 1, 1898, Spanish land batteries fired from Manila and Sangley Point, without effect. Dewey coolly withheld response until within 5,500 yards of Montojo's numerically larger but weaker squadron. At 6:19 A.M. Dewey turned to *Olympia's* captain and spoke the words destined to become an American catchphrase: "You may fire when ready, Gridley."

For about an hour the American ships steamed up and down the Spanish battle line, firing as they went. The Spanish returned heavy fire, and by the end of the battle every U.S. ship had been struck, but none seriously. After five passes Dewey ordered fire checked and moved out of range. Later, newspapers claimed tongue in cheek that the commodore had called off the fight temporarily so that the men could have breakfast. They did eat, but the lull had been occasioned by disturbing tidings from Gridley. "At 7:35 A.M.," Dewey explained, "it had been erroneously reported to me that only 15

rounds per gun remained for the 5-inch rapid-fire battery. I ceased firing and withdrew the squadron for consultation and a redistribution of ammunition, if necessary. . . . " (5-19).

The sailors were grateful for the unexpected opportunity to relax above decks (5-20), but on the bridge anxiety prevailed until a check proved that the report was erroneous—fifteen rounds per 5-inch gun had been *fired*, not *remained*. What is more, no ship had suffered serious damage, and there had been no fatalities. So, at approximately 11:16 A.M., much heartened, the Americans resumed action.

The Spanish squadron, however, had already been badly mauled. At about 7:00 A.M., the flagship *Reina Cristina* (5-21), the best of Montojo's ships, had, in Dewey's words, "made a desperate attempt to leave the line and come out to engage at short range, but was received with such galling fire, the entire battery of the *Olympia* being con-

5-19 Commodore Dewey, wearing a rakish, nonregulation touring cap, confers with Capt. Charles V. Gridley, *Olympia's* commanding officer, and his chief of staff, Cmdr. Benjamin P. Lamberton, during the 7:35 A.M. to 11:16 A.M. lull in the action at Manila Bay.

5-20 In this artist's depiction, sailors on board *Olympia*, some stripped to the waist, take a breather during the lull in the action on May 1.

centrated upon her, that she was barely able to return to the shelter of the point. The fires started in her were not extinguished until she sank." "With great sorrow," Montojo had to transfer his flag to the gunboat *Isla de Cuba. Reina Cristina*'s captain, Luis Cadarso, died heroically, attempting to rescue survivors.

Another Spanish captain put up a valiant fight—Alonso Morgado Pita de Viego of the unprotected cruiser *Castilla* (5-22). She was as ready as possible and opened fire about 5:00 A.M., but the wooden-hulled, lightly armed ship proved no match for the American return fire. Soon she was in flames and sinking, with the loss of twenty-five dead and more than thirty wounded. Pita de Viego received permission to abandon ship and transferred the remaining crew to shore. A third ship, the unprotected cruiser *Don Antonio de Ulloa* (5-23), was also sunk suffering losses of eight killed and ten wounded.

Total Spanish casualties amounted to 161 killed and 210 wounded. The American casualties

5-21 The Spanish unprotected cruiser *Reina Cristina*, flagship of the Spanish squadron, later sunk off Cavite

5-22 The sunken Spanish unprotected cruiser *Castilla*. The U.S. protected cruisers *Olympia* and *Baltimore* can be seen in background (left).

5-23 The iron-hulled unprotected cruiser *Don Antonio de Ulloa*, sunk off Cavite

were only 9 wounded, eight on board *Baltimore* and 1 on *Boston*. At 12:15 the Spanish hoisted a white flag, and Dewey called off the bombardment. Gunboats *Isla de Luzon* and *Isla de Cuba* (5-24) were scuttled and set on fire. Later both would be raised and refitted and would serve the U.S. Navy for several years. Photograph 5-25 shows *Isla de Luzon*'s flooded main deck, fire damage aft, two of her main battery of four 4.6-inch guns and

her sister ship, *Isla de Cuba*, in the background. Photograph 5-26 shows her mainmast fallen to starboard and one of the ship's main batteries of 4.7-inch guns is visible. Fire has eaten away the wooden decking.

The gunboat *Petrel's* captain detailed a party of seven men under her executive officer, Lt. Cmdr. Edward M. Hughes (5-27), to destroy these and other Spanish ships. Among those thus destroyed,

5-24 The gunboats *Isla de Luzon* (left) and *Isla de Cuba*; the latter was the ship to which Admiral Montojo shifted his flag after American gunfire disabled his flagship *Reina Cristina*.

5-25 Looking aft on board *Isla de Luzon*. *Isla de Cuba* lies in background.

5-26 Looking forward from *Isla de Cuba*'s poop deck.

5-27 Lt. Cmdr. Edward M. Hughes, executive officer of the gunboat *Petrel*, who led a seven-man party from that ship to burn Spanish men-of-war off Cavite

in addition to *Isla de Luzon* and *Isla de Cuba*, were the gunboats *Don Juan de Austria*, *General Lezo*, *Marqués del Duero*, and *El Cano* (5-28). The demoralized Spanish sailors, who watched numbly from shore, allowed Hughes and his men to carry out their mission of destruction without hindrance.

With what deep grief and dismay the Spanish viewed the scene that met their eyes on the after-noon of May 1, one can only imagine (5-29). In contrast, the Americans were gratified and thankful that material damage to U.S. ships was minimal (5-30). Even more important, U.S. casualties included no fatalities (5-31).

Two days after the naval battle, a detachment of U.S. Marines from the cruiser *Baltimore* took over the Cavite navy yard, site of the Spanish naval arsenal (5-32). About this time, Dewey took an un-

5-28 Party of sailors from the gunboat *Petrel* boarding and setting Spanish gunboats afire off Cavite, May 1, 1898

5-30 A sailor on board *Olympia* poses by the dented plate on the starboard side of the superstructure, just forward of the second 5-inch gun sponson. This was the only scar the cruiser received (faintly visible to the right of the rope).

5-29 Panorama of destruction off Cavite. The transport *Isla de Mindanao* (left), gunboats *Isla de Luzon* and *Velasco* (right); U.S. gunboat *Petrel* is in the distant background. Note *Isla de Luzon*'s blackened stern, and one of her four 4.7-inch Hontoria rifles.

5-32 Lt. Dion Williams, USMC, and a portion of the Marine guard from the protected cruiser *Baltimore*, which occupied the Cavite navy yard on May 3, 1898

5-31 One of *Olympia*'s mascots, this parrot, is said to have lost a leg at Manila Bay.

5-33 First reinforcement for Dewey's squadron came in the form of the protected cruiser *Charleston*.

characteristically obtuse action. The Spanish authorities in Manila refused him permission to use the cable to Hong Kong, so Dewey ordered it cut. This effectively cut him off from telegraphic contact with his superiors in Washington. The only way to get his dispatches through was to send them to Hong Kong via *McCulloch*, which sailed for that port on May 5.

Before communications had been severed, however, the Spanish captain general had sent a dispatch to Madrid claiming that Montojo's ships had inflicted severe losses on the American squadron. Montojo's reports considerably dampened that assessment, but the Spanish press printed only what the government wanted re-

leased. Consequently, at the outset, both Spain and the United States had no real idea what had taken place. To the Americans, Dewey's silence seemed ominous. So, when *McCulloch* reached Hong Kong on May 8 and sent off Dewey's dispatches, his country exploded with joy.

Ironically, the first major engagement of the Spanish-American War had taken place not in Cuba, the center of attention, but thousands of miles away in a spot many Americans probably would have had trouble locating on a map. It did not matter; Dewey had smashed the Spaniards and the United States saw him as the hero of the hour. "Dewey mania" swept the country. McKinley gave him a well-deserved promotion to rear admiral, parents christened newborn babies Dewey, and his face appeared on uncounted mugs, plates, and even chair backs.

Too practical to allow this adulation to go to his head, Dewey knew he was in a somewhat awkward position. As he informed Secretary Long, he could take Manila any time but could not hold it without troops. He needed reinforcements as quickly as possible. Fortunately for the United States, men were quickly and efficiently assembled, supplied, and transported across the Pacific. Three converted passenger liners carrying supplies and 2,500 soldiers proceeded to the Phil-

ippines, escorted by the protected cruiser *Charleston* (5-33). En route the convoy stopped at Guam on June 20 and took possession of the island from the Spanish garrison, whose commander was unaware that Spain was at war with the United States. Other convoys followed.

One of the transports, the 5,080-ton *City of Pekin*, is shown in photograph 5-34 en route to Manila. Another ship headed for the Philippines in late June was the monitor *Monadnock* (5-35). After a slow trans-Pacific voyage via Hawaii she reached her destination on August 16, 1898, after the close of hostilities.

5-34 The transport *City of Pekin*, one of the three troop transports convoyed by *Charleston*, en route to Manila

5-35 The monitor *Monadnock*, as seen from the collier *Nero*, en route to the Philippines, demonstrates the seagoing qualities for which monitors were justly infamous—her main deck awash.

The Spanish planned to send reinforcements to the Philippines, and a fleet under Admiral Manuel de la Cámara y Libermoore sailed eastward toward the Philippines through the Mediterranean toward the Suez Canal. The most powerful ship in the squadron was the heavily armed battleship *Pelayo* (5-36). In the armored cruiser *Carlos V* (5-37) Cámara had another excellent vessel whose capabilities, along with those of *Pelayo*, bothered Dewey considerably. Admiral Cámara also possessed a number of less formidable ships, such as the merchant cruiser *Patriota* (5-38). Cámara's threat to Dewey never materialized, however, because the British refused the Spanish coaling privileges at the Suez Canal, leaving Cámara no choice but to return to Spain.

5-36 The battleship *Pelayo* moored at Port Said, Egypt, between June 22 and July 11, 1898

5-37 The armored cruiser *Carlos V* at Port Said, on either June 22 or July 1, 1898. Vessel in left background is either the *Colón* or *Covadonga*, merchant steamships requisitioned to naval service. At right is the stern of the naval steamship *Buenos Aires*.

5-38 The armed merchant cruiser *Patriota*, Port Said, on either June 22 or July 11, 1898. She had been acquired as the steamship *Normannia* from the Lloyd Line.

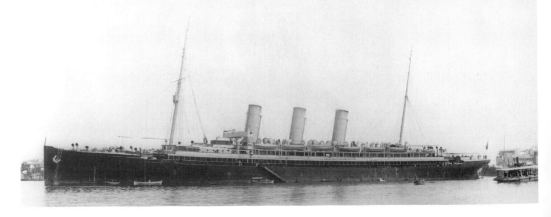

The Blockade

Back on April 21, 1898, McKinley had formally declared a blockade of all ports on Cuba's north coast between Cárdenas and Bahía Honda. Cienfuegos on the south coast was also blockaded, but not on a regular basis. McKinley selected these particular areas because they had railway connections with Havana that could be used to keep the capital supplied. If matériel were landed elsewhere, lack of transportation plus the activity of the insurgents would make delivery to Havana exceedingly difficult, if not impossible.

Early on the morning of April 22 the North Atlantic Squadron under Vice Admiral William T. Sampson left home waters to enforce the blockade. Americans greeted the prospect of action with excitement and displays of patriotism, as did the Spanish loyalists in Cuba.

Sailors in general disliked blockade duty because it involved all the hardships and inconveniences of sea duty without what Secretary Long called "the exhilaration of combat." Long added,

"Many devoted officers and crews, from the beginning of the war to the end, rendered most valuable and conscientious service without opportunity for winning distinction in battle."

The blockade achieved success at the outset when the gunboat *Nashville* stopped the unarmed merchantman *Buena Ventura* on April 22 (6-1). *Buena Ventura* was en route from Pascagoula, Mississippi, to Holland with a cargo of lumber, and, having no idea that the United States and Spain were at war, her captain courteously hoisted the Spanish flag in salute. *Nashville* answered with a shot across *Buena Ventura*'s bow— the first one of the war—and quickly rerouted the freighter to Key West. Four days later, *Nashville* racked up another first when she captured the Spanish mail steamer *Argonauta* off Cienfuegos, taking the first Spanish prisoners of war (6-2).

The next day, April 27, Sampson's flagship, the armored cruiser *New York*, with the protected cruiser *Cincinnati* and monitor *Puritan*, bom-

6-1 The gunboat *Nashville* (right) inaugurates the blockade, stopping the Spanish merchantman *Buena Ventura*, April 22, 1898

6-2 Rufus F. Zogbaum's sketch of the first Spanish prisoners of war, captured on board the Spanish mail steamer *Argonauta* on April 26, 1898

barded Matanzas to prevent completion of a new shore battery at Punta Gorda, drawing fire from enemy guns for the first time in the conflict (6-3). A gunner on board *Puritan* aimed at the circle of smoke from the Spanish gun; his shot went right through the middle, destroying the cannon. An awestruck British observer called this "the most marvelous exhibition of accurate gunnery in the history of gun fighting." Richard Harding Davis, on board *New York* to report on the war, recorded that during the action "from below came the strains of the string band playing for the officers' mess . . . ." So far operations off Cuba had an air of unreality, more like an unusually relaxed war game than the real thing, but American sailors *had* been under fire for the first time. That some would fall in battle was only to be expected.

Thus far, neither an American sailor nor a Marine had died in combat. That would soon change. On May 11, the unprotected cruiser *Marblehead* and gunboat *Nashville* arrived off Cienfuegos to cut the telegraph cables linking that port with the outside world (6-4). Tars and leathernecks in steam cutters and sailing launches from the two warships, both of which provided heavy covering fire for the operation, carried out their hazardous mission (6-5) under disturbingly accurate Spanish gunfire. "I can not speak in too high terms of

the officers and men engaged in the four boats in cutting the cables," wrote Cmdr. Bowman H. McCalla, senior officer present in the engagement. "Their work was performed with utmost coolness and intrepidity under most trying circumstances." Among the fifty-two Medals of Honor (the most awarded for a single naval engagement in the entire war) given to those who fought at Cienfuegos were those that went to Canadian-born brothers Willard D. (6-6) and Harry H. Miller (6-7), from *Nashville.*

Despite American valor, the operation was unsuccessful. The men had been able to cut only two of the three cables; communication with Spain via Jamaica remained uninterrupted for the duration of hostilities. For the first time in the war, U.S. military forces had suffered casualties. Nine men had been wounded; from *Marblehead*—Apprentice First Class Ernest Suntzenich and Pvt. Patrick Reagan, USMC—later died of their wounds.

Still other losses came at Cárdenas, located some eighty miles east of Havana, later the same day. Only a short time before, on May 8, the torpedo boat *Winslow* had reconnoitered that port, prompting Spanish gunboats to get under way to engage her. *Winslow* drew the largest of them into range of the gunboat *Machias*'s 5-inch guns. Un-

6-3 Artist Henry Reuterdahl's impression of the bombardment of Matanzas on April 27, 1898

THE CABLE CUTTING EXPEDITION AT CIENFUEGOS.

6-4 Lithograph depicting the cutting of one of the telegraph cables linking Cienfuegos and Havana, May 11, 1898

6-5 Launch from the gunboat *Nashville*, used in severing the cable at Cienfuegos

6-6 Seaman Willard D. Miller of the gunboat *Nashville*, a Canadian, earned the Medal of Honor for cutting the Spanish telegraph cable off Cienfuegos.

6-7 Seaman Harry H. Miller served alongside his brother Willard in *Nashville* and also received the Medal of Honor for heroism off Cienfuegos.

der fire briefly from the larger ship, the Spanish craft retired immediately.

Winslow paid a return visit to Cárdenas on May 11 to join the gunboat *Wilmington* and revenue cutter *Hudson* in an attempt to capture the Spanish warships previously sighted in the port. As she neared the harbor to determine the exact location of the enemy vessels, *Winslow* came under murderous fire from a shore battery that, in short order, disabled one engine, wrecked the steering gear, and jammed her rudder.

Reduced to the expedient of maneuvering by "alternately backing and steaming ahead—zigzagging out, as it were," *Winslow*'s commanding officer, Lt. John B. Bernadou (6-8), shrugging off a flesh wound, tried to extricate his ship from her predicament. Despite the enemy's concentrated fire, *Winslow* managed to reach *Hudson*. Lt. Frank

6-8 Lt. John B. Bernadou, commanding officer of the torpedo boat *Winslow*, wounded in action at Cárdenas

6-9 Artist's depiction of the revenue cutter *Hudson* towing the disabled torpedo boat *Winslow* out of range of Spanish guns off Cárdenas, Cuba, May 11, 1898

B. Newcomb, Revenue Cutter Service, brought *Hudson* alongside, and, after one towline parted, the plucky tug towed the crippled warship out of harm's way (6-9).

Winslow had suffered extensive material damage (6-10), but while ships can be repaired, making good the loss in human life is more difficult. Of her crew of twenty-one, three had been wounded and five killed. Among those slain was Lieutenant Bernardou's executive officer, Ens. Worth Bagley, a Naval Academy graduate who had served less than three years (6-11). Bagley was the first—and only—U.S. naval line officer killed during the war with Spain. Lieutenant Bernardou eulogized him as "a gallant officer, whose bravery and stainless record will ever be held in remembrance by his brethren."

The deaths of Bagley and Oiler John Varveres, Firemen First Class John Dneefe and George B. Meek, and Cabin Cook Elijah B. Tunnell, however, had not been in vain. In silencing the shore batteries, the American fire from the three ships had killed seven Spanish soldiers, in addition to two

sailors on board the armed tug *Antonio Lopez*, which, along with the smaller gunboat *Lealtad*, sank in shallow water off the wharf to which they had been moored at the start of the action. The action by *Winslow*, *Wilmington*, and *Hudson* meant that the Spanish navy would no longer threaten that portion of the blockade.

Blockading Cuban ports and preventing supplies from reaching Cuba was all well and good, but an even greater priority for the North Atlantic Squadron lay in finding and destroying the Spanish fleet, under Admiral Cervera, which had sailed west from the Cape Verde Islands on April 29. Rumors abounded as to his destination. Some believed he would turn south to attempt to intercept and sink *Oregon* somewhere near Rio de Janeiro; others that he would take his ships around the Horn to cross the Pacific to relieve the Philippines; still others believed rumors that his squadron had been sighted off Canada, speeding toward New England and American East Coast ports. If Cervera had been aware of that gossip, it might have accorded him a few moments of grim

6-10 *Winslow*'s after conning tower, showing indentations from Spanish shell hits

6-11 Ens. Worth Bagley, photographed at Key West, Florida, circa March 1898

humor. Better than anyone else, he knew he would be lucky to emerge from the conflict with any of his ships still afloat.

The rumors, however, did not beguile U.S. naval strategists, who, factoring in likely French and Dutch attitudes at Martinique and Curaçao, respectively, correctly reasoned that Cervera more than likely was headed for Puerto Rico. Rather than simply wait for Cervera to show up, the U.S. Navy searched vigorously for his fleet. Until the Spanish ships could be located and engaged, sending an expeditionary force to Cuba by sea was fraught with peril.

Vice Admiral Sampson believed the Spanish would put in to San Juan probably on May 8 and hoped to be there when they arrived. Thus, on May 4, he gambled on his hunch by detaching the battleships *Iowa* and *Indiana*, armored cruiser *New York*, cruisers *Detroit* and *Montgomery*, monitors *Amphitrite* and *Terror*, torpedo boat *Porter*, collier *Niagara*, and armed tug *Wompatuck*. A group of ships, however, no matter how powerful, can proceed as a body only as fast as its slowest

unit. Machinery trouble plagued *Indiana* while the two wallowing, low-lying monitors had to be towed by *New York* and *Iowa*. The result was that Sampson reached his destination on May 12, four days behind schedule, to find no Spanish warships in port.

Unable to seize San Juan, Sampson bombarded it to determine the strength of the shore batteries. In the action, which lasted a little over two and a half hours, neither side suffered major material damage, although a 6-inch shell struck *New York*, killing one man and wounding four; shell fragments wounded three men on board *Iowa*.

Sampson returned to Key West in *New York* on May 18, finding Commodore Winfield S. Schley's Flying Squadron already there. The rest of Sampson's squadron arrived the following day and soon began replenishing their coal supplies. Hypothesizing that Cervera was bound for Cienfuegos, Sampson dispatched Schley's force to blockade that port.

Meanwhile, a Cuban insurgent sympathizer in the telegraph office at Havana had sent positive word on the night of May 19 that Cervera's warships had arrived at Santiago. Confirming word came the following night. Arriving off Martinique on May 12 (the same day Sampson bombarded San Juan), Cervera had not been able to obtain coal there and pushed on for Curaçao, where the Dutch authorities had allowed him only 600 tons. The Spanish then steamed directly for Santiago, which they reached on May 19.

Commodore Schley, however, on reaching Cienfuegos, erroneously concluded that Cervera's force was *there*. Even when Sampson's orders reached him, Schley delayed acting on them. Cmdr. Bowman McCalla of the cruiser *Marblehead* sent a reconnoitering party ashore on May 24; friendly Cubans informed them that Cervera (who, ironically, that day was contemplating shifting his squadron to San Juan) was in fact not at Cienfuegos after all. Only then did Schley move toward Santiago, arriving off the port on May 26, only to order his force to retire to Key West for coal, defending his decision on the grounds of rough seas. Sharply ordered to return to Santiago to blockade the port, Schley did so, reaching there

on May 28; Sampson, with the rest of the fleet, joined him on June 1. The naval forces arrayed off Santiago had bottled up the Spanish squadron.

Even before he had arrived off Santiago, Sampson had proposed preventing Cervera's ships from escaping by sinking a collier to obstruct the channel narrows. To determine the feasibility of the operation, he sought out Assistant Naval Constructor Richmond P. Hobson, who "manifested a most lively interest in the problem." After careful study, the twenty-seven-year-old naval constructor proposed to rig the collier *Merrimac* (which, in her brief career had proved prone to breakdowns and thus was no great loss to the fleet) (6-12) with explosives and, after anchoring her in place across the channel, blow out the plating along one side of the ship and sink her. Recognizing "that the success of the undertaking absolutely depended upon the man who was to be intrusted [*sic*] with its execution," Sampson allowed Hobson to command the hazardous operation himself.

The Alabama-born Hobson (6-13) had entered the Naval Academy at fifteen and had graduated,

6-12 The collier *Merrimac* fitting out for service, Norfolk Navy Yard, April 23, 1898

6-13 Assistant Naval Constructor Richmond P. Hobson

as its youngest member, at the head of the class of 1889. His aptitude for the nuts and bolts of the naval profession had been such that he was sent to England for three years to study naval architecture. On his return, he had taught postgraduate courses in naval construction at the Naval Academy.

Hobson's final calculations called for a crew of seven men. The tide of patriotism and sense of adventure was running so high that obtaining the required number of sailors proved easy. "Enough officers and men volunteered," Sampson later observed, "to man a hundred *Merrimacs*." Eager sailors stepped forward in droves—140 on board *New York* alone. Of those selected, three came from *Merrimac*'s original complement: Coxswain Osborn W. Deignan, Machinist First Class George P. Phillips, and Water Tender Francis Kelly. From the flagship *New York* came Hobson, Gunner's Mate Third Class George Charette, and Coxswain Randolph Clausen. *Brooklyn* contributed Chief Master-at-Arms Daniel Montague, while *Iowa* supplied Coxswain John E. Murphy.

After time-consuming preparations on June 2, the same day that Sampson deployed his ships in a semicircle off Santiago, Hobson's expedition got under way at 3:00 A.M. on Friday, June 3. A steam launch from *New York*, with Naval Cadet Joseph W. Powell and a five-man crew, followed *Merrimac* to take off the pilot and *Merrimac*'s chief engineer, who had volunteered to stay on board to leave the collier's machinery "in condition to complete the trip without further care." Powell took off those two men and then stood by to rescue survivors after the vessel sank. As soon as *Merrimac* entered the channel, however, the Spanish sighted her and riddled her with heavy fire from all calibers, which succeeded in shooting away the rudder, without which the ship could not steer to her intended grave (6-14); she thus sank in an unintended position. Naval Cadet Powell looked for survivors but, after a diligent search under fire, returned to *New York* empty-handed.

Hobson and his gallant band, however, had survived the flurry of bullets and shells and, clinging to a raft, had been captured after daybreak by a Spanish launch; Admiral Cervera himself helped Hobson from the water. Later that day, the admiral sent Capt. Joaquín de Bustamente, his chief of

6-14 Artist's conception of *Merrimac* being sunk off Estrella Point, near the channel to Santiago harbor, by heavy Spanish gunfire

staff, under a flag of truce to inform Sampson that Hobson and his men were alive and well and were "honored prisoners of war." The Spanish tug Colón took Bustamente out to the armed yacht *Vixen*, which conveyed him to *New York*, where he personally communicated the news to Sampson and his flag captain, Capt. French E. Chadwick (6-15). Less than a month after this chivalrous visit, Bustamente, an eminent electrician and inventor of the torpedo that bore his name, would fall mortally wounded in the defense of Santiago.

Although the attempt to block the channel had failed, that fact did not dim the luster of the try. "I can not myself too earnestly express my appreciation of the conduct of Mr. Hobson and his gallant crew," Sampson wrote on June 3. "I venture to say that a more brave and daring thing has not been done since Cushing blew up the *Albemarle* [during the Civil War]." Later, the Americans learned from a Spanish deserter from the unarmored cruiser *Reina Mercedes* (not part of Cervera's squadron, having been in Cuban waters since 1896) that *Merrimac* actually had sunk too far

inside the harbor to block the entrance (6-16 and 6-17). Americans in general, however, wholeheartedly added Hobson and his brave shipmates to a growing pantheon of naval heroes.

As a postscript, a little more than a month later, on the afternoon of July 6, General William R. Shafter and Governor General Ramón Blanco y Erenas agreed on an exchange of prisoners that released the *Merrimac* crew. Three Spanish officers, blindfolded before being led through the American lines, caught the attention of the troops in the trenches (6-18). Like a flash fire, the word spread along the line—Hobson was being exchanged! After a long wait, three men on horseback appeared, one in naval uniform (6-19).

As a man, the U.S. soldiers leaped to attention; some doffed their hats in a sweeping salute (6-20). Stephen Crane, war correspondent and author of the novel *The Red Badge of Courage*, an observer to the scene, initially suffered a twinge of disillusionment when Hobson began bowing to the left and right like an actor acknowledging applause, but all seemed right again when the wagon ap-

6-15 Capt. Joaquín de Bustamente, Cervera's chief of staff (center), calls on Rear Admiral Sampson (foreground) and the *New York*'s commanding officer, Capt. French E. Chadwick (right), on board Sampson's flagship, the *New York*.

6-16 View from El Morro shows the sunken *Reina Mercedes* in the foreground and the tip of *Merrimac*'s masts and stack.

6-17 Close-up of the wreck of the collier *Merrimac*, sunk near the channel at Santiago

6-18 Spanish prisoners—1st Lt. Pius Giner Gastaminza, of the 6th Battalion, Lower Peninsula Infantry among them—on their way to be exchanged for Hobson and his *Merrimac* crew, near Santiago.

6-19 Hobson leads his men back to American lines. The Spanish released them in exchange for captured Spanish soldiers.

6-20 As Hobson's men pass, one soldier respectfully doffs his campaign hat while another rushes up to the rear of the wagon that is carrying (front to rear) Gunner's Mate First Class George Charrette, Machinist First Class George F. Phillips, and Water Tender Francis Kelly.

peared, carrying the enlisted men, grinning in the sheer pleasure of freedom (6-21). Each of the eight men involved in the daring exploit ultimately received the Medal of Honor.

The idea of establishing a base at Guantánamo Bay, located about forty miles east of where Cervera's fleet lay holed up, to coal ships in shel-

tered waters had been contemplated before Sampson had arrived. Guantánamo offered virtually the only harbor where ships could take refuge during the hurricane season and would obviate the coaling problem that had so concerned Schley. On June 6, Sampson sent *Marblehead* and auxiliary cruiser *Yankee* to reconnoiter

6-21 As word of the arrival of Hobson's crew spreads, American soldiers throng around them to welcome them back.

the lower bay under the direction of Cmdr. Bowman H. McCalla (6-22), who had overseen the cable-cutting off Cienfuegos. More important for the task at hand, however, McCalla possessed as good, or better, an understanding of Navy–Marine Corps operations as any of his contemporaries. His concern for the welfare of Marines moved one leatherneck to write admiringly, "There was not a man in our command who did not like him."

Marblehead (6-23) and *Yankee* drove the Spanish gunboat *Sandoval* into the upper reaches of Guantánamo Bay, out of range of the American guns, to Caimanera. Then McCalla put ashore twenty Marines from his ship's guard and forty each from *Oregon* and *New York* to scout the area. Under Capt. Mancil C. Goodrell, USMC, commander of *New York*'s marine guard, these were the first U.S. ground forces to set foot on Cuban

6-22 Cmdr. Bowman H. McCalla, captain of the unprotected cruiser *Marblehead*, who supervised the landings at Guantánamo Bay in June 1898

6-23 The cruiser *Marblehead* as she appeared during the war with Spain

soil. They destroyed the cable station at Playa del Este before they returned to their respective ships via *Yankee*. *Marblehead* and the collier *Sterling* took possession of the lower bay on June 8.

It was not until June 10 that the 1st Marine Battalion, 648 men strong, came ashore at Fisherman's Point from the transport *Panther* (6-24) under the command of Lt. Col. Robert W. Huntington, USMC, a Civil War veteran (6-25). The Marines trudged up the steep hill with their "tents, tent-poles, cooking outfits, ammunition, intrenchment

[*sic*] tools, etc." and established "Camp McCalla," named in honor of the operation's commander (6-26). There would be no rest for the weary, however, for the leathernecks on outpost duty that night heard Spanish soldiers moving about in the dense undergrowth beyond their lines.

At 5:00 P.M. on June 11, the battalion suffered its first casualties when Spanish forces attacked an outpost, killing Pvts. James McGolgan and James Dumphy, USMC (6-27). The detachment sent to support them found scant trace of the enemy,

6-24 The transport *Panther* (seen here as the passenger steamship *Venezuela* under way in New York Harbor) transported Marines to Guantánamo Bay.

6-25 Lt. Col. Robert W. Huntington who had fought at Bull Run, commanded the 1st Marine Battalion.

6-26 Camp McCalla, named in honor of *Marblehead*'s captain, atop the hill (background, left) overlooking the beach

who returned on five different occasions after nightfall (6-28) and into the next day to harass Camp McCalla with fire from different directions. Each time the Marines responded "with promptitude and courage" to the Spanish thrusts (6-29).

During the predawn action of June 12, Assistant Surgeon John B. Gibbs (6-30), who had given up "a fine practice in New York" to become a Navy doctor, was shot through the head and died instantly. His death, a shipmate later wrote, "cast a gloom over the whole command, as he was a most popular officer, liked by all, [whose] services were very much missed and the battalion could ill afford to lose them." Pvt. Frank Keeler,

6-27 Graves of "The First Martyrs," Pvts. James McGolgan and James Dumphy and Acting Assistant Surgeon John B. Gibbs, among the tents of Camp McCalla, late June 1898. Spanish pressure on the entrenchments had compelled the Marines to bury their dead inside the camp itself.

6-28 Artist's conception of Marines at Guantánamo, aided by the cruiser *Marblehead*'s searchlights, repelling the first Spanish attack on the night of June 11–12, 1898

6-29 Artist F. C. Yohn's depiction of Marines returning Spanish fire at Guantánamo being reinforced by their shipmates from camp. While Yohn's depiction of the Marines' headgear (undress caps) is correct, he inaccurately shows them in blues—they landed clad in brown linen campaign uniforms.

6-30 Assistant Surgeon John B. Gibbs, the only naval medical officer to die in the Spanish-American War

USMC, summed up Gibbs's loss more succinctly: "We were all sorry to lose the sergeon [*sic*] for the other one left [Surgeon John M. Edgar], was no earthly good." Others, however, later noted that Edgar, after having seen his assistant fall at his side to the fatal Mauser bullet, "continued his work alone, doing it thoroughly and well."

Later on the morning of June 12, the Marines suffered four more casualties, one dead and three wounded, before they moved their tents and matériel to the opposite side of the hill, facing the bay, and then dug in across the south front of their camp. That day, some sixty insurgent troops, under Col. Alfredo Laborde, arrived. "Excellent woodsmen, and fearless," the Cubans, because of their detailed knowledge of the local terrain, proved of "great assistance" to Huntington's Marines. Moreover, Private Keeler observed, the arrival of the Cubans "gave us courage when we were able to look upon those who we were fighting for." Commander McCalla had them provided with U.S. Navy uniforms (6-31).

That same day, sailors from the collier *Abarenda*, under Lt. Stephen Jenkins, had erected a flagstaff on the foundation of a Spanish blockhouse destroyed by *Yankee* on June 7, and *Marblehead* supplied the flag, which was raised amidst cheers (6-32).

"Persistent and trifling attacks" continued on the night of June 12–13; in the predawn darkness of June 13, First Sergeant Henry Goode, USMC, the battalion sergeant major, was killed, but the Marines managed to subdue the Spanish fire "without loss or difficulty" as the day wore on. The next morning the battalion suffered its last fatality when a private fell off an embankment and died of a broken neck.

To relieve the pressure on the Marines, Commander McCalla, at the suggestion of the Cubans, ordered an assault against Cuzco Well, located six miles from Guantánamo and the only Spanish water supply within a twelve-mile radius. The well's existence, McCalla believed, had enabled the enemy to keep up their "annoying attacks" that had so far vexed the leathernecks. On June 14, Capt. George F. Elliott, USMC, command of the expedition having devolved to him because of Huntington's illness, set out with Companies C

6-31 While a fatigued leatherneck takes a breather seated on the lip of a wheelbarrow, two Cuban soldiers, attired in U.S. Navy white duck uniforms, stand nearby.

6-32 1st Lt. Henry L. Draper, USMC, adjutant of the First Marine Battalion, raises the Stars and Stripes over Camp McCalla.

and D, augmented by a force of fifty Cubans and supported by guns of the dispatch boat *Dolphin* (6-33).

At one point in the action, *Dolphin* began shelling an area occupied by the leathernecks. Sgt. John H. Quick, USMC, promptly signaled the ship in time to prevent a friendly fire tragedy, alternately joining his shipmates in "using his [Lee-Metford] rifle with equal judgement"—an exploit that earned him the Medal of Honor (6-34). Many

6-33 The dispatch boat *Dolphin*, as she appeared in the 1890s

6-34 Diorama depicting the heroism of Sgt. John H. Quick, "with the utmost coolness" signaling the dispatch boat *Dolphin*, which is mistakenly shelling 2d Lt. Louis J. Magill's platoon during the Cuzco Well fight, June 14, 1898. Quick was awarded the Medal of Honor.

6-35 This leatherneck, his Lee-Metford rifle across his lap, rests in the shade of a rude lean-to at Camp McCalla, June 17, 1898. More practical campaign hats arrived four days later.

Marines, Captain Elliott reported later, "fired as coolly as at target practice, consulting with each other and their officers as to the range." Sunstroke proved to be a potent enemy that day. Some twenty-three men had to be sent on board *Dolphin* for treatment.

After a brisk and spirited engagement, Elliott's men and their Cuban allies had driven off a nu-

6-36 Overall view of Guantánamo Bay, June 26, 1898, showing the Cuban camp (lower left); ships sheltering in the harbor include the gunboat *Bancroft*, cruisers *Detroit* and *Marblehead*, and battleship *Oregon*.

merically superior Spanish force—estimated later to have been at least four companies of regular infantry and two companies of irregulars, some five hundred men—and destroyed the well. The expedition relieved Camp McCalla, and Huntington considered the captain's gallantry and skill essential to the success. Ultimately, Elliott, a future commandant of the corps, was advanced three numbers on the promotion list for "eminent and conspicuous conduct under fire."

Although some six thousand Spanish soldiers remained near Guantánamo, they never seriously threatened the battalion again. The leathernecks' camp medical record put the army's to shame. Only 2 percent of the command suffered illness, and not a single Marine died of sickness. The Marines could relax (6-35), having secured the first beachhead on Cuban soil. Thenceforth, U.S. ships of all types could base there in safety for the remainder of hostilities (6-36).

The United States Invades Cuba

On May 26, 1898, the War Department directed General Shafter to prepare to load 25,000 men and supporting artillery onto transports, serving notice that the unpleasant but safe period of training in Tampa was about to end. This was only a small portion of the total available manpower, however, because the War Department hoped to keep the majority training in Florida until autumn, when the yellow fever season would be over in Cuba.

The miscellaneous assortment of vessels that constituted the transports was not ready to load. The onset of war found the army with neither transports nor landing craft. It was necessary to purchase or lease steamers to act as troop carriers. The War Department soon discovered that the much more efficient Navy Department had already skimmed off the cream of the ships available from the American merchant marine, which was already in poor shape. The twenty-nine steamers and several light craft that the army settled for were mostly coastal freighters. They could handle cargo but had to be modified with bunks for men and stalls for horses and mules.

On May 31, Shafter received confirming word from Secretary of War Russell A. Alger. He was directed to put his command on board transports, "proceed under convoy of the navy to the vicinity of Santiago de Cuba . . . to capture or destroy the garrison there," and, with the Navy's help, "capture or destroy the Spanish fleet. . . ." The order ended, "When will you sail?" This message seemed to imply that Alger expected Shafter to march his troops briskly on board, load their equipment, and take off in a day or two.

This sparked a rush to break camp and move to the piers. Photograph 7-1 shows the 9th Infantry engaged in this process; photograph 7-2 shows soldiers of the 21st Infantry placing their equipment aboard a train headed for Port Tampa's piers, there to be loaded onto the transports *Saratoga* and *City of Washington*. Photograph 7-3 shows a trooper easing his horse into a livestock car, although most of the cavalry's mounts had to be left behind because of lack of space on board the ships.

The facilities at Port Tampa were singularly ill-suited for a massive embarkation. The wharf (7-4) could handle only two ships at once, with six others awaiting their turn in the channel. Rail connections between the railroad terminal at Tampa and the dock area were even less satisfactory. The

7-1 Tents come down at Tampa as the 9th Infantry breaks camp and makes ready for embarkation to Cuba.

7-2 While one of their company officers looks on, men of the 21st Infantry load their equipment into boxcars.

7-3 A trooper from Troop C, 2d Cavalry, coaxes a horse into a Seaboard Air Line livestock car bound for the SS *Morgan*.

7-4 The finger piers and jetties of Port Tampa

army had laid down some rail tracks, but not enough to bypass the single, one-way commercial line. It did not help that Tampa's promoter, Morton F. Plant, ran excursion trains on the rail to enable tourists to see the activity at the port.

Soon the chaos was such that it appeared beyond solution (7-5); it was certainly beyond the ability of Shafter and his aides to resolve. In fact, no U.S. Army officer had any experience in preparing for a major overseas movement. Unwilling

7-5 Railway cars carrying men and equipment of the Cuban expedition transform the docks at Port Tampa into a logistical nightmare.

to admit how bad conditions were, Shafter informed the War Department that he probably could depart in three days. He must have known this was unrealistic; not until the next day were the ships even ready to receive supplies.

General Nelson A. Miles reached Tampa on June 1 and found an indescribable mess, not only with transportation but also with supplies. Missing invoices and bills of lading in many instances forced officers to break into the cars to determine what they contained.

On June 6—already beyond the deadline—it became apparent that the transports could not accommodate 25,000 men and their equipment; in fact, they could take no more than 18,000 or 20,000. Shafter had to concede that the troops, even thus reduced, could not board ship until the next day.

On that morning, June 7, Sampson wired the Navy Department that with 10,000 troops Santiago could be taken "within forty-eight hours." If the troop movement was delayed, though, guns from the Spanish fleet might be added to the city's defenses. He urged "immediate army movement." To stress the urgency, President McKinley wired

Shafter that time was "the essence of the situation. Early departure of first importance."

Shafter had not been idle. His 300-pound bulk perched precariously on two cracker boxes, he had been personally supervising the loading, using a packing box as a makeshift desk. Troops were finally beginning to move (7-6 and 7-7). The transport *Segurança* had been selected to carry Shafter's V Corps headquarters, along with the 1st Infantry (7-8) and the Signal Corps Balloon Detachment. After an interminable wait, the 9th Infantry, the 1st Division headquarters, and a

7-6 Infantrymen trudge across the tracks toward what they hope will be their assigned transport.

7-7 The colors of the 1st Infantry move toward the long-anticipated embarkation onto the transports.

7-8 Lt. Col. William Bisbee (left), sword resting on his right shoulder, leads his 1st Infantry onto the gangplank of the transport *Segurança*, which is just out of view at left.

battalion of the 10th Infantry boarded the *Santiago* (7-9). Some regulars, accustomed to the army procedure of "hurry up and wait," stacked arms and fell asleep (7-10).

This was no orderly embarkation, with units awaiting their turn and on signal marching up the gangways to settle in their assigned positions. Not until the evening of June 7 were the commanders

7-9 The 9th Infantry boards the *Santiago*. The Krag rifle of the first sergeant at left is protected by a canvas covering.

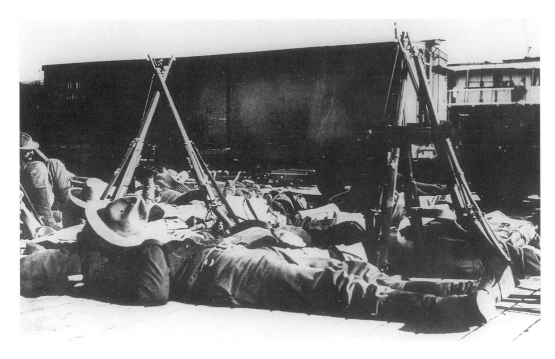

7-10 The long wait proved to be too much for these regulars.

advised that they would be sailing the next morning, and indeed they never did receive formal word; the news spread via the military grapevine.

Theodore Roosevelt did not need to be told what would happen. With 25,000 men ready to embark and ship space for only 18,000 to 20,000, there would be a stampede to the transports. When the train intended to carry the Rough Riders did not show up, he commandeered a train of empty coal cars and got his men to the port on time, grimy but ready to go. He learned that their ship was the *Yucatan* and discovered that it had also been assigned to the 2d Cavalry and the 71st New York Volunteers. He hurriedly rounded up his men and took possession of the *Yucatan*, holding the gangway against all comers (7-11). Eventually

7-11 The Rough Riders from the 1st Volunteer Cavalry, without their horses, clamber on board the *Yucatan* for the sea journey to Cuba.

he allowed four companies of the 2d Infantry aboard. Inadvertently, he had done the 71st a favor—it was moved to the *Vigilancia*, a better billet than the *Yucatan*.

Almost all of the cavalry, including the Rough Riders, fought dismounted for the duration of the campaign (7-12). Later some wags changed the name "Roosevelt's Rough Riders" to "Wood's Weary Walkers."

In addition to the living cargo—officers, enlisted men, civilians, horses, and mules—the transports carried artillery (7-13), wagons, ammunition, and other supplies (7-14).

A list of the units bound for Cuba, with their commanding officers, appears in chart 7-15. It was early afternoon of June 8 when the ships finally began to move. Loaded transports such as the *Comal*, carrying Company I, 7th Infantry, and Batteries E and K, 1st Artillery (7-16), joined a procession of vessels moving out into Tampa Bay. Among them was the *Seneca* (7-17), weighed down with men and equipment from the 8th Infantry, 2d Massachusetts Volunteers, and Brig. Gen. William Ludlow's brigade staff. Awaiting their turn were two transports, the *Knickerbocker* and *City of Washington* (7-18). The latter had been in Havana

7-12 Horses and mules await their turn to board the ships moored to the docks at Port Tampa.

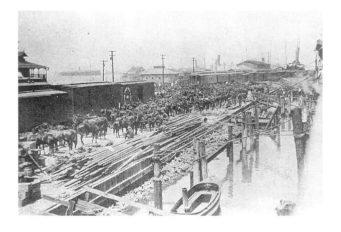

7-14 Ammunition and supplies being loaded into a vessel's cargo hold at Port Tampa

7-13 With the assistance of a ship's cargo crane, men load Cuba-bound light artillery pieces onto a transport (either the *Berkshire* or *Comal*).

7-15 The units that made up the Santiago expedition:

V Corps—Maj. Gen. William R. Shafter

1st Div.—Brig. Gen. Jacob F. Kent

1st Brig.—Brig. Gen. H. S. Hawkins

6th Inf.	—Lt. Col. Egbert
16th Inf.	—Col. Theaker
71st N.Y. Vols.—Col. Downs	

2d Brig.—Col. E.P. Pearson   3rd Brig.—Col. C.A. Wikoff

2d Inf. —Lt. Col. Wherry	9th Inf. —Lt. Col. Ewers
10th Inf.—Lt. Col. Kellogg	13th Inf.—Lt. Col. Worth
21st Inf. —Lt. Col. McKibbin	24th Inf.—Lt. Col. Liscum

2d Div.—Brig. Gen. Henry W. Lawton

1st Brig.—Brig. Gen. William Ludlow

8th Inf.	—Maj. Conrad
22d Inf.	—Lt. Col. Patterson
2d Mass. Vols.	—Col. Clark

2d Brig.—Col. N. A. Miles   3d Brig.—Col. A. R. Chaffee

1st Inf. —Lt. Col. Bisbee	7th Inf. —Col. Benham
4th Inf. —Lt. Col. Bainbridge	12th Inf.—Lt. Col. Comba
25th Inf.—Lt. Col. Daggett	17th Inf. —Lt. Col. Haskell

Cavalry Division—Maj. Gen. Joseph Wheeler

1st Brig.—Brig. Gen. S. A. Sumner   2d Brig.—Brig. Gen. S. Young

3d Cav. —Maj. Wessels	1st Cav. —Lt. Col. Viele
6th Cav.—Lt. Col. Carroll	10th Cav. —Maj. Norvell
9th Cav.—Lt. Col. Hamilton	1st Vol. Cav. —Col. Wood

Indep. Brig.—Brig. Gen. John C. Bates

| 3d Inf. —Col. Page |
| 20th Inf. —Maj. McCaskey |
| 2nd Cav. —Maj. Rafferty (1 Sqdn.) |

7-16 Ready to commence their voyage into the Caribbean, loaded transports move out into Tampa Bay. The *Comal*'s stern is visible at center.

7-17 The transport *Seneca* (designated Army Transport No. *5*) moves out into Tampa Bay. Note the men climbing onto her masts.

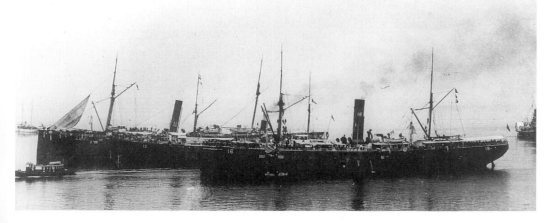

7-18 The *Knickerbocker* (left) and *City of Washington* (right) lie alongside each other in Tampa Bay before the voyage to Cuba.

harbor when *Maine* exploded and had helped rescue survivors.

No sooner had the ships gotten under way than Shafter, about to board the *Segurança*, received a cable from Alger: "Wait until you get further orders before you sail." Whatever Shafter may have thought of this latest example of hurry-up-and-wait, he stoically recalled the transports and boarded the *Segurança* to await developments.

Alger's cable had been sent in response to a report that one of the U.S. Navy's converted yachts, *Eagle*, had spotted what it believed to be two Spanish warships—an armored cruiser and a torpedo boat destroyer—in San Nicolás Channel, off Cuba's northern coast. Old fears of Spanish naval prowess were awakened, and the navy wasted five precious days searching before deciding that the sighting had been a mistake.

That period proved one of undiluted suffering for the troops, immobilized under a south Florida summer sun in poorly ventilated holds. Many of these vessels depended entirely on ventilator cowls and the forward motion of the ship to circulate fresh air below decks. No movement meant no fresh air. The animals soon began to die and had to be unloaded. The officers feared for the health of their men. Roosevelt, furious, wrote, "We are in a sewer; a canal which is festering as if it were Havana harbor." The delay, however, had its positive side, in that it gave Shafter time to load more equipment, including medical supplies, which did not reach Tampa until June 12.

After two days spent replenishing the ships' water supply and reloading the horses and mules, the expedition finally set out on June 14 (7-19). Among the ships leaving in the morning was *Matteawan*, with her complement of 32 officers and 734 men of the 20th U.S. Infantry, Troops D and F of the 2d Cavalry, and headquarters of the Independent Infantry Brigade (7-20). Another

7-19 Under way at last! One of the lead vessels in the Santiago expedition steams ahead, leaving a large number of vessels in her wake.

7-20 The transport *Matteawan*, her "designating number" *26* on her funnel, steams toward Cuba.

early starter was *City of Washington* (7-21), with troops of the 24th U.S. Infantry and the 1st battalion of the 21st U.S. Infantry. A larger group left that afternoon and evening, including *Saratoga* (7-22), with the 13th Infantry and the main body of the 21st Infantry on board. The *Segurança* was the last to depart.

Soldiers who were quick enough, or strong enough, to secure berths were fortunate and at least could enjoy a fairly comfortable night's sleep. Photograph 7-23 demonstrates the common practice at that time of retouching photographs and painting in the faces blurred by movement during the long exposure times required.

As was the custom, several foreign military attachés, including representatives of Germany, Austria, Russia and Italy, accompanied the expedition as observers (7-24). Like Admiral Sampson's approach to Puerto Rico, Shafter's convoy was tied to the speed of its slowest components, in his case one transport towing a barge, another towing a schooner. The ships had difficulty keeping in line, and stragglers fell behind and became lost. Gunboats of the navy convoy had to round them up, reminding Richard Harding Davis of alert collies caring for stupid sheep. The transports kept their running lights on even when opposite clearly visible Spanish positions. The attachés toyed with the possibility of Spanish torpedo boats picking off transports as if they had been mechanical ducks in a shooting gallery. "Perhaps no nation but Spain," a British reporter noted, "would have allowed us a passage unmolested." The transports rendezvoused with the navy off Santiago on June 20.

Later that day Sampson came to the *Segurança* to pick up Shafter in his gig and take him ashore at Aserradero, a town in rebel hands, to meet with Cuban General Calixto García Íñiguez. Much de-

7-22 The *Saratoga* steams into the Gulf of Mexico during the voyage to Cuba.

7-21 Troops crowd the upper decks of the transport *City of Washington*, en route to Cuba.

7-23 Having grabbed the first available berths, these lucky soldiers have a proper place to sleep.

7-24 Foreign military attachés on board a Cuba-bound transport, likely the *Segurança*

pended on the mutual good will of the Americans and the Cuban rebels. The McKinley administration had not recognized the insurgents' provisional government; hence no formal alliance existed. No joint headquarters was established, there would be no exchange of officers, no Cuban rebels would serve in American units, and vice versa. All depended on cooperation at the top level.

They discussed strategy, and perhaps it was only natural that each commander thought in terms of his own branch of the service. Sampson wanted the troops to land on each side of the Santiago harbor entrance and storm the heights to capture Morro Castle and Socapa. Then the Navy would clear the channel of mines and sweep in to demolish the Spanish fleet as Dewey had done in the Philippines. Needless to say, Shafter took an exceedingly dim view of thus unnecessarily sacrificing his men—"the height of folly" he later called Sampson's strategy. Guantánamo Bay would have provided a perfect debarkation point but would have involved crossing forty miles of rugged terrain, with the threat of yellow fever hanging over every mile. Shafter feared yellow fever considerably more than he did the Spanish.

With Cuban concurrence, he proposed to land initially at Daiquiri, some fifteen miles east of Santiago. García recommended Daiquiri, although it had minimal docking facilities, because the Spanish garrison there numbered no more than three hundred. From Daiquiri the Americans could move up to Siboney, about halfway between Daiquiri and Santiago. The navy's part would be to shell Spanish positions from Cabañas to Daiquiri. The navy also loaned Shafter a number of officers, whose advice and assistance were invaluable, because no one in Shafter's command had any experience in amphibious landings.

The operation began on June 22 and could have been a disaster. First, Spanish general Arsenio Linares y Pomba, in charge of the defense of Santiago, predicted that the Americans would land at Daiquiri and Siboney. Second, both sites were readily defensible. Roosevelt estimated that five hundred Spanish soldiers could have stopped the invasion. The Spanish pulled out before trouble began, however, burning buildings behind them (7-25).

This proved fortunate for the Americans because the operation was, as Roosevelt observed disgustedly, "a scramble." Many of the transport skippers refused to move near shore, and many troops had to disembark as far out as five miles into boats towed by launches (7-26). This task fell to the armed lighthouse tender *Suwanee* and the tugs *Osceola* and *Wompatuck*. Each man was

7-25 Burned by the retreating Spaniards, the railway station at Daiquiri lies in ruins.

7-26 Launches tow the first of the U.S. troops ashore at Daiquiri on June 22, 1898.

7-27 The Rough Riders disembark from the *Yucatan*.

loaded down with a blanket roll, three days of field rations, canteens filled with water, and a hundred rounds of ammunition. Horses and mules were pushed overboard to swim to shore. Only five or six drowned, but the survivors, already in poor shape from their long incarceration in the sweltering holds, where fifty had died, were exhausted by the time they made it to shore.

Among the early arrivals was *Yucatan*, bearing the Rough Riders (7-27). Landing facilities were poor (7-28 and 7-29), and the surf was running high, but amazingly only two men were lost. A

7-28 The steam lighter *Laura* pulls alongside the rickety pier at Daiquiri to offload her human cargo, a host of transports in the distance. At center lies the *D. I I. Miller*, waiting to disembark a battalion of the 7th Infantry.

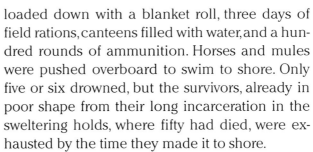

7-29 American soldiers at Daiquiri climb out of a small launch at the head of the pier.

Rough Rider officer, Capt. "Bucky" O'Neill, plunged in to rescue them, but they had perished almost immediately.

Brig. Gen. Henry W. Lawton's 2d Division, Brig. Gen. John C. Bates's Independent Brigade, and Maj. Gen. Joseph "Fighting Joe" Wheeler's dismounted cavalry division disembarked with orders to advance immediately on Siboney. They lost no time in preparing to do so (7-30). Despite the disorganized nature of the proceedings, some six thousand of the projected sixteen thousand troops landed in the first two days. By early on June 23, troops began moving toward Siboney (7-31 and 7-32).

Originally, Shafter ordered his entire force to be unloaded at Daiquiri, but since the Spanish had been driven away from Siboney, he decided to land Brig. Gen. Jacob F. Kent's 1st Division there to expedite bringing his entire operation ashore. Shelling of Siboney preceded the landings. The

7-30 Units consolidate, collect their equipment, and await the long-anticipated advance into the Cuban interior.

7-31 Firmeza, a mining town north by northwest of Daiquiri, lay in the path of the Americans advancing from Daiquiri.

7-32 Panoramic view of Siboney from the south. The tents indicate that the landings there on June 23 predated these photos.

armed lighthouse tender *Suwanee* "entered close to the beach and shelled it thoroughly" on June 22 (7-33), while the 4-inchers of the gunboat *Bancroft* (7-34) also contributed, much to the satisfaction of her officers and crew (7-35). Considerable damage was done to the town (7-36).

On June 23, transports were in position awaiting the word to unload (7-37) and then sent troops ashore in small boats (7-38). In contrast to the sea at Daiquiri, that at Siboney was quiet, and

those already on shore could wade out to help their comrades (7-39). In a scene that would become familiar, Cuban refugees flocked to the Americans for protection and food (7-40). Exactly what they thought those transports at sea and those new tents on land (7-41) meant to them, no one can say.

Views of the coast (7-42) and harbor (7-43) show how easily the Spanish might have thwarted American attempts to land at Siboney had they

7-33 The armed lighthouse tender *Suwanee* under way off Siboney, passing the auxiliary cruiser *St. Louis* (left) and armed yacht *Vixen* (right)

7-34 Crewmen on board the gunboat *Bancroft* watch as her port 4-inch guns bombard Siboney, June 22, 1898.

7-36 Smoke rises from burning buildings at Siboney during the bombardment by the gunboats *Annapolis*, *Bancroft*, and *Helena* and the armed yacht *Hornet*, June 22, 1898.

7-37 Transports await word to unload at Siboney off the southeast coast of Cuba.

7-35 "Made a bull's eye that time!" The pleased expression on the officer's face (center) mirrors *Bancroft*'s accurate fire at a Spanish blockhouse at Siboney, June 22, 1898. Note the 6-pounder guns to port and starboard, with sandbags piled around the base of the cage mounts.

7-38 The landings at Siboney commence on June 23 as U.S. troops come ashore in small boats. Soldiers in the distance have taken off their trousers to lend assistance in the surf, which appears calm.

7-39 Bare-legged Americans, along with several Cubans, assist in landing operations, while a Cuban soldier stands guard. The *Orizaba* lies at center, disembarking the 22d Infantry and Shafter's siege artillery battalion.

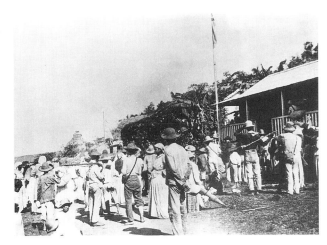

7-40 Frightened and hungry, Cuban refugees flood onto the grounds of the U.S. headquarters at Siboney to escape the fighting. The roof of the blockhouse appears in the distance at left.

7-41 Transports at anchor off Siboney, with tents in the middle foreground

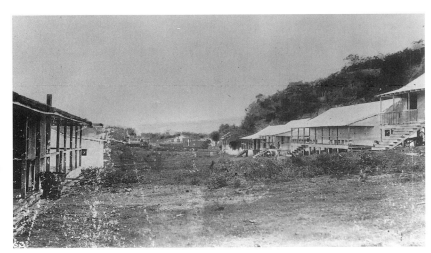

7-42 A view of the coastline looking through the small village of Siboney, which lies along the road leading to the interior

7-43 A view of the harbor at Siboney seen from the heights, which extend inland about three-quarters of a mile

concentrated troops there instead of electing to refuse battle. Small as Siboney was, it had limited rail and road connections with Santiago (7-44 and 7-45), so the troops began moving toward their destination (7-46)—and toward an unexpectedly fierce engagement.

Evidently, Shafter's purpose was to consolidate his strength at Siboney in case of counterattack from the Spanish at Santiago. This made considerable sense, because debarkation was not yet com-

pleted. However, Shafter was still on board *Segurança*, and the ranking general on shore was Maj. Gen. Joseph Wheeler (7-47). Physically, Wheeler was the opposite of Shafter, standing five feet two inches tall and weighing only 110 pounds. He had been one of the Confederacy's most renowned generals, however, and after the Civil War's end he had been an active and respected congressman. He did not relish inaction. When Cuban General Demetrio Castillo informed

7-44 The railroad bridge at Siboney, which the Spanish attempted unsuccessfully to destroy

7-45 Leading out of Siboney toward Santiago, the main road passes an abandoned Spanish blockhouse.

7-46 Pack mules of an ammunition train move to the front along the main road from Siboney to Santiago.

7-47 Maj. Gen. Joseph Wheeler, commanding the cavalry division of V Corps

Wheeler that some 1,500 Spanish troops under General Linares had come together at Las Guásimas, a village located in a range of hills straddling the main road from Siboney to Santiago (7-48), about three miles to the north, he decided to act instead of continuing on to Siboney. At Las Guásimas General Linares had deployed his troops in three lines:

General Antaro Rubin—Overall command and first line

1st line—Porto Rico Regiment—3 companies

—1 horse-drawn cannon company
   Major Alkakñiz

2nd line—San Fernando Regiment—3 companies placed short distance behind the rear line

—1 engineering company

—80 guerrillas

Colonel Borry

3rd line—Talavera Regiment—5 companies

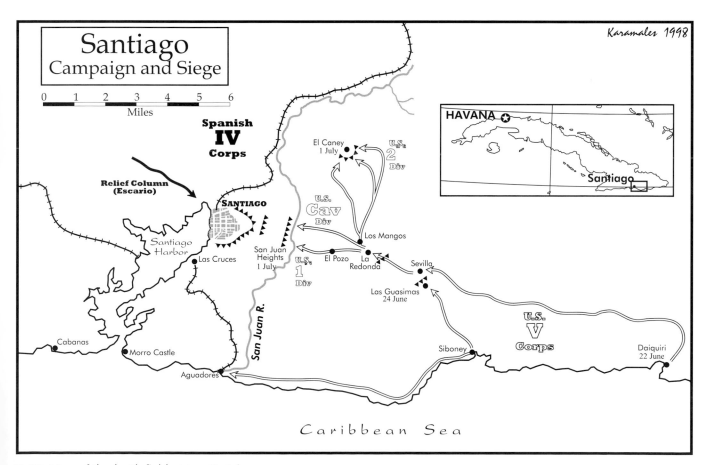

7-48 Map of the battlefield at Las Guásimas

7-50 Artillery train in a narrow defile at Las Guásimas.

7-49 Men from the 9th Infantry build a road to the front near Las Guásimas.

placed at Redonda farther west to guard against attacks against the flank and rear —30 mounted guerrillas

General Castillo's Cuban troops had made several unsuccessful attempts to breach the Spanish position on the afternoon of June 23. Meanwhile, Wheeler took over command from Brig. Gen. Henry W. Lawton and ordered Brig. Gen. Samuel B.

M. Young to make a "reconnaissance in force." Young's plan was to have one squadron each of the 1st and 10th Cavalry press forward on the main road. One of the latter's officers was Lt. John J. Pershing, whose nickname of "Black Jack," which would endure throughout his distinguished career, no doubt came from his service with the 10th. Colonel Wood, with two squadrons of Rough

7-51 Col. Leonard Wood, commander of the 1st Volunteer Cavalry, who, along with the 1st and 10th Cavalry, engaged the Spaniards at Las Guásimas

7-52 Resting place of seven Rough Riders, including Sgt. Hamilton Fish, killed during the fighting at Las Guásimas

Riders from the 1st Volunteer Cavalry, would move along a trail to the left of the road. Plans to coordinate the attack with Castillo, however, fell through.

The march started at daybreak on June 24. The dense jungle and narrow trail made progress agonizingly slow (7-49 and 7-50). Young opened the fight at 8:00 A.M., firing down the main road with a Hotchkiss mountain gun. His regulars pressed slowly under cover of brush toward the crest of the hill. Meanwhile, Wood (7-51) and his Rough Riders worked their way up the jungle on the left, running into the Spanish advance guard at 7:30 A.M. The first to fall was Sgt. Hamilton Fish, grandson of President U.S. Grant's secretary of state and one of several young aristocrats who had joined the Rough Riders. He was buried with six of his comrades (7-52). Shortly after Fish's death, Capt. Allyn K. Capron fell mortally wounded—the first American Army officer to lose his life during the campaign (7-53). His father, Capt. Allyn K. Capron,

Sr., a renowned artillerist, would die of yellow fever in September. [To the best of our knowledge, this was the only American father and son duo to give their lives in Cuba.]

Eventually, the Rough Riders crashed into the Spanish right flank and rear and, together with the mass of regulars advancing from the front, forced the Spanish from the position (7-54). The Spanish immediately retired toward Santiago. The Americans lost sixteen killed and fifty-two wounded (7-55). Spanish losses totaled ten killed and eighteen wounded. The Americans had just under one thousand men engaged, the Spanish about one thousand five hundred out of two thousand present. The results—giving up a position where they outnumbered the American force two to one— did not auger well for the Spanish. Wheeler had been fortunate. Had Linares chosen to make a stand instead of pulling out, the outcome could have been very different (7-56 and 7-57).

7-53 Lonely grave at Siboney of Capt. Allyn K. Capron of the 1st Volunteer Cavalry, killed at Las Guásimas on June 24, 1898—the first American Army officer to lose his life during the Santiago Campaign

7-54 Road through the jungle at Las Guásimas where the 1st and 10th Cavalry suffered most of their casualties

7-55 Wounded Rough Riders walking down the trail left of the main road leading to Las Guásimas

Col Miles
comdg 2d Brig

Please return to harbor near from which you started draw rations and move to that point—on road taken by Genl Chaffee—

Enemy retreated to Santiago. Our loss here about 30 killed and 100 wounded. Several officers killed and wounded..

Respy
Lawton
Brig Genl

7-56 The first message, sent to General Miles by General Lawton, concerning the action at Las Guásimas, the expedition's initial engagement on Cuban soil

7-57 The sundial at Sevilla, Cuba, a landmark that veterans of Young's 2d Brigade would always associate with their first battle at Las Guásimas.

CHAPTER 8

The Santiago Campaign—Part I

For six days after the action at Las Guásimas, the Americans did nothing to follow up their advantage. General Shafter ordered Major General Wheeler not to conduct another "reconnaissance in force," and in fact no one carried out reconnaissance of any kind. Nor did anyone set about the important task of clearing the pathways leading to Santiago. The Americans could clearly see the Spanish strengthening the defenses at El Caney and San Juan Hill, but with no orders to the contrary, the troops spent their time hunting for food, trying to cadge tobacco from the Cubans, and resting. A naval bombardment could have disrupted the Spanish preparations and seriously damaged their fortifications, but Shafter did not ask Rear Admiral Sampson for such support. Shafter's own heavy guns could not be unloaded and had to be left behind.

By June 26, American supply problems began to manifest themselves. Some troops had been without rations for days, resulting from the failure of the regimental commanders to carry out the order to take three days' rations before disembarking. Some regiments had taken no rations whatsoever. Further, the wagons landed at Siboney on June 24 served only to clog the roads, which were in execrable condition. This resulted in a shortage of supplies on the front lines.

Brigadier General Arsenio Linares had about ten thousand Spanish troops in Santiago, with little prospect of reinforcement. Some military experts have faulted Linares for not bringing in his outlying troops, who were posted throughout the province, but his problem was not a simple one. The insurgents, while not in complete control of the land routes, dominated the area enough to hamper seriously any Spanish troop movements, and the American blockade precluded reinforcement by sea. Moreover, Santiago was near starvation. No food had been received since April, and a sizable influx of soldiers would place a heavy strain on the food reserve. Also, Linares's soldiers had not been paid for over a year.

Linares planned to defend Santiago in three stages—an outer skirmish line that could offer no more than token resistance; a second, stronger

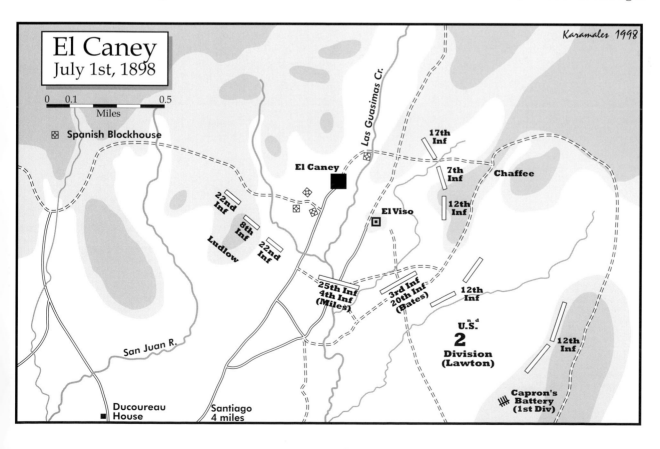

8-1 American troop dispositions at El Caney at approximately midday on July 1, 1898

line of fortifications, including El Caney, Kettle Hill, and San Juan Hill, with a few additional fortified points; and third, the city of Santiago itself. Linares knew that reinforcements might be on the way. On June 22 Col. Federico Escario, with 3,600 men, left Manzanillo, headed for Santiago.

Manzanillo was only forty-five miles away, but that was a long distance given the state of Cuban roads. In fact, Escacío did not arrive until July 3.

Learning of this movement, Shafter decided to attack Linares as soon as possible. After coming ashore on June 29, he established his headquar-

8-2 The most advanced American outpost along the road to Santiago on the afternoon of June 30

8-3 Determined to lighten his load, a private from the 7th Infantry, Chaffee's brigade, Lawton's division, entrusts his worldly possessions (except for his Krag and ammunition belt!) to a donkey during the advance toward Santiago.

8-4 Panoramic view of the town of El Caney, seen from Fort El Viso

ters one mile east of El Pozo, where the army lay concentrated along the Sevilla-Santiago Road. He believed that he could wait no longer for further reinforcements. Accordingly, on June 30, on receiving intelligence on the Spanish positions at El Caney to the north and San Juan Heights to the west, Shafter decided to move on both objectives early on July 1.

Shafter's plan was to detach Brig. Gen. Henry Lawton's division (with Capt. Allyn Capron's battery) north to El Caney, where it would dispose of the threat to the army's right flank there, wheel to the west, and then rejoin Brig. Gen. Jacob Ford Kent and Wheeler (on Wheeler's right) for a three-division assault on San Juan Heights (8-1).

The health of the American troops, which would deteriorate during the siege, was still excellent. By June 30, the ration supply situation had sorted itself out. Greatly encouraged by the fight at Las Guásimas, the Americans were eager for battle (8-2). As always in Cuba, the march was difficult and took longer than expected (8-3). Shafter had ordered all units to march at the same time and, as the roads were no more than eight or ten feet wide, the result was a major traffic jam.

Suddenly, illness required changes at the command level. Wheeler and Brig. Gen. Samuel Young both came down with fever. Brig. Gen. Samuel S. Sumner took over for Wheeler, while Col. Leonard Wood replaced Young. This left Roosevelt in command of the Rough Riders, to his gratification. Shafter had intended to lead the fight in person, but his obesity, gout, and heat prostration left him in not much better shape than his two ailing cavalry generals, and he was unable to leave his tent at his newly established headquarters near El Pozo.

First objective of the campaign was the village of El Caney (8-4), which Shafter and Lawton expected to take after no more than two hours' fighting. El Caney, named for the palm-thatched huts common to the area, lay on one of a series of hills rising between the fingers of the San Juan River and Las Guásimas Creek north of the Sevilla-Santiago road. The Spanish position there consisted of four wooden blockhouses, a loopholed church in the village, and a stone fort, which the defenders dubbed El Viso, or "the petticoat," for unknown reasons—perhaps in honor of the ladies of El Caney. In front of and connecting the blockhouses were deep, narrow trenches and rifle pits.

To oppose Lawton's division, the Spanish had in position only three companies of the Constitución Regiment and one company of dismounted

cavalry, all commanded by Brig. Gen. Joaquín Vara del Rey—520 men to face Lawton's 6,600.

During the afternoon of June 30, Capron changed the position of his battery of four 3.2-inch guns to a point south of El Caney to support Lawton's attack (8-5). American forces at El Caney included Lawton's division (Ludlow's, Miles's, and Chaffee's brigades); the independent brigade of Brig. Gen. John C. Bates (just up from Siboney); and Capron's battery—approximately 6,600 men. Chaffee took position facing El Viso to the right. Ludlow marched to the southwest side to cut off the retreat of the Spanish garrison. Initially, Bates and Miles were held in reserve.

To Capt. Allyn Capron (8-6) fell the honor of opening the battle, which was fitting, because his son had been killed at Las Guásimas. He began with a bombardment at 6:30 A.M. on July 1 (8-7). Then Chaffee's brigade opened fire, followed shortly by Ludlow. The Spanish return fire was so heavy that the Americans could advance no closer than within 600 yards of the Spanish position. Lying totally exposed and hugging the earth, the Americans nonetheless pressed forward, making every

8-5 Capron's battery changes position from El Pozo to a point south of the Spanish position at El Caney on the afternoon of June 30.

8-6 Battery commander Capt. Allyn Capron, whose son became the first army officer casualty of the war at Las Guásimas, one week before the engagement at El Caney

8-7 Capron's battery in action near El Caney on July 1

effort to drive the Spanish from their entrenchments. A Spanish staff officer said, "I have never seen anything to equal the dash and courage of those Americans. . . . Their gallantry was heroic."

The officers were no less directly engaged. Ludlow had a horse shot out from under him. By noon it was clear that the estimate of a two-hour fight had been a gross error and that it was time to call up the reserves. Photograph 8-8 was probably taken before the call-up at 1:00 P.M. of the units commanded by Brigadier General Bates and Colonel Miles.

The Spanish forces under Vara del Rey (8-9) were proving themselves first-class soldiers. They had no artillery but were taking a heavy toll with their Mausers, while their smokeless powder concealed their individual positions. Gradually, Chaffee (8-10) edged closer to El Viso from the east and Ludlow crept toward the entrenchments and blockhouses on the southwest side. Miles took position on Ludlow's right; Bates drew up between Miles and Chaffee (8-11).

At 2:00 P.M., with his assault schedule in tatters, Shafter ordered Lawton to withdraw and support

8-8 General Lawton (left center) inspects the American lines before El Caney and confers with General García (left) and the two brigadiers— Ludlow (right center) and Chaffee (right)—commanding Lawton's left and right flanks, respectively.

8-9 Brig. Gen. Joaquín Vara del Rey, commander of El Caney's gallant defenders

8-10 Col. Adna R. Chaffee

the attacks, which by then were under way, on San Juan Heights. His order read in part: "I would not bother with little block-houses; they cannot harm us . . . "

Considering that Shafter had believed El Caney important enough to allot a good third of his forces to its capture and that Spanish forces in this particular "little block-house" had been hitting U.S. soldiers at an alarming rate, that phrase must have seemed almost obscene at the time. Lawton was shocked; to withdraw would be to acknowledge defeat, and his troops were so closely engaged that it would have been dangerous to break off. He requested Shafter's permission to keep on with

the fight at El Caney, but before an answer could be received the climax had come.

At about 2:30 P.M., Capron's battery found the range on El Viso and began to breach the walls with repeated direct hits. Ludlow saw his chance and ordered a final assault on the fort by Chaffee from the east (8-12) and by Bates and Miles from the south. Chaffee's men dashed across the open field and assaulted and captured the stone block-house on the summit (8-13). In twenty minutes the brigade lost twenty-seven killed and seventy-three wounded.

Bates (8-14) and Col. Evan Miles had led their brigades against El Viso (8-15) from the left (8-16).

8-11 View of the El Caney battlefield looking west from the position held by Chaffee's brigade on the right flank of Lawton's division

8-12 An unidentified officer with field glasses watches developments during the assault on El Caney.

8-13 The eastern face of El Viso, assaulted by the men of Chaffee's brigade

8-14 Brig. Gen. John C. Bates

The town itself (8-17) was the next objective of Ludlow (8-18a) and Miles (8-18b). Even though El Viso had fallen, there was still fighting in the town and around the blockhouses to the southwest. Spanish troops had loopholed and fortified the historic old church, which they held until Capron's artillery drove them out (8-19).

While rallying his men in the last stages of the fighting at El Caney, Vara del Rey was shot through both legs and then through the head as his men bore him away. His body was left behind, and the Americans buried him with military honors. Ludlow took temporary charge of the Spanish leader's spurs and sword. At the surrender of

8-15 Stone fort at El Viso, viewed from southwest of El Caney, there assaulted by the brigades of Bates and Miles

8-16 View looking north toward one of the El Caney blockhouses with barbed-wire entanglements, situated on the road leading southwest from El Caney, advanced on by Ludlow's right and Miles's left

8-17 View looking north into El Caney from the blockhouse, which lay in the line of Ludlow's and Miles's advance

Santiago, Shafter presented them to Gen. José Vasquez Toral, to be returned to Vara del Rey's family, a gesture that pleased the Spanish. Señora Vara del Rey could not have concurred with John Hay's assessment of the conflict as "a splendid little war." She had lost not only her husband but also two sons at El Caney.

At about 5:00 P.M., some one hundred Spanish escaped to the west. Spanish losses totaled more than 50 percent—235 killed and wounded and 120 taken prisoner (8-20). American losses were 81 killed and 360 wounded.

The survivors were glad of the chance to stack arms and rest (8-21). Someone, inspired by Henry V's Agincourt speech in William Shakespeare's play, penned a poem in appreciation of their prowess:

> We were not many, we who stood
> Before the leaden sleet that day.
> Yet many a gallant spirit would
> Given half his years, if he but could
> Have stood with us at El Caney.

The Americans had cause for pride, because they had fought bravely. But it had been no easy victory. Outnumbering the Spanish nearly nine to one, they had taken the Spanish positions only with the greatest difficulty.

The fight at El Caney still raged when the main body of Shafter's forces began their assault on the San Juan Heights (8-22). It was a strange battle, fought without overall direction. Too ill to lead in person, Shafter (8-23) commanded from his tent, issuing orders through his adjutant general, Lt. Col. E. J. McClernand. Roosevelt, whose opinion of Shafter's generalship was sulfurous, considered him "criminally incompetent. . . ." He added, "The battle simply fought itself."

If manpower were the sole consideration, the battle for the San Juan Heights should have been a walkover. The Americans had approximately eight thousand troops against slightly more than three hundred Spaniards in the first line, who did most of the fighting. The Spanish were positioned in three lines, as follows (8-24):

1st Line (321 men)
     Talavera Regiment—2 companies
     Porto Rico Regiment—1 company
2d Line (410 men)
     Talavera Regiment—3 companies
     2 artillery pieces
3d Line (140 mounted guerrillas)

8-18 Brig. Gen. William Ludlow and Col. Evan Miles

8-19 The plaza in El Caney

8-20 Roundup of Spanish prisoners in the wake of the El Caney battle

8-21 American infantrymen rest after stacking arms on a portion of the El Caney battlefield late in the afternoon of July 1.

8-22 Troops near General Shafter's headquarters press ever closer toward Santiago, circa June 30, 1898.

8-23 Before proceeding farther toward the front, General Shafter and his staff pause to water their horses.

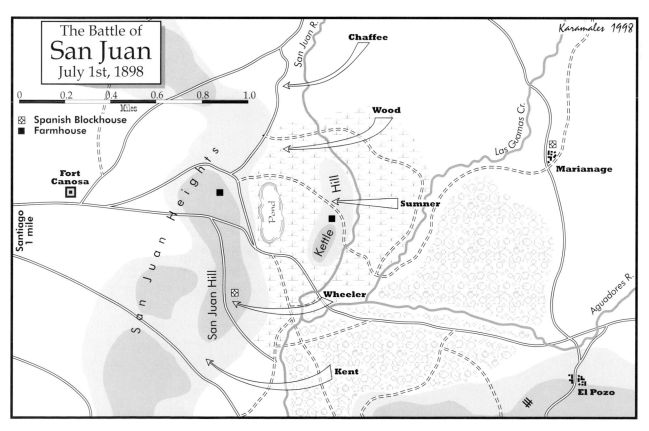

The Battle of **San Juan** July 1st, 1898

Karamales 1998

Spanish Blockhouse
Farmhouse

8-24 Map of the San Juan battlefield

As always in battle, however, manpower was not the sole criterion. The Spanish had fortified the hills well with trenches and barbed wire. El Caney

8-25 El Pozo (The Well), Shafter's headquarters during the Battle for San Juan Heights, as seen from the position of Grimes's battery

8-26 The guns of Capt. George S. Grimes's light field artillery commence firing at Spanish positions on San Juan Heights.

and San Juan Heights presented examples of the trench warfare that would reach its culmination in World War I. Merely reaching the scene of battle was hazardous in the extreme, involving a march of over a mile on a narrow road through jungles full of snipers, fording the small San Juan River, and then crossing an open space offering no cover for about 400 yards before facing the enemy, entrenched on high ground.

Early on the morning of July 1, Wheeler's and Kent's divisions lay at El Pozo (8-25), awaiting what proved to be an illusive "quick victory" at El Caney. Rather than wait for Lawton, Shafter ordered the other two divisions forward to engage Linares before he could attempt to reinforce the garrison at El Caney. Shafter's orders directed Wheeler's division (temporarily commanded by General Sumner of the 1st Brigade) to deploy across the San Juan River north of the Sevilla-Santiago Road, with Kent's division deployed similarly to the south. Then both divisions were to drive forward and take possession of the heights.

Capt. George S. Grimes's light field artillery, consisting of four 3.2-inch guns, opened fire at 8:20 A.M. (8-26), using black powder charges, which not only revealed the battery's position but also obscured the view of the target. Moreover, Grimes's guns were too far away to do any damage. After an artillery duel with the Spanish, the exchange broke off at approximately 10:00 A.M. (8-27).

8-27 Col. John Jacob Astor watches the effect of American artillery fire on the Spanish positions.

After Grimes ceased fire, Sumner (8-28) led his men down the main road, forded the Aguadores River, filed to the right, deployed in the shelter of a sunken road, and awaited Kent's deployment to the south. Sumner retained command, although Wheeler had ordered an ambulance to take him to the front. Once there, the sights and sounds of battle seemed to act on him like a powerful restorative. Soon he called for his horse and actively participated.

Reconnaissance had been sketchy, and the Americans attempted to rectify the omission by sending up an observation balloon (8-29). Lt. Col. George Darby, Shafter's chief engineer, and Lt. Col. Joseph Mansfield of the Signal Corps were in the basket (8-30). Results were mixed. On the positive side, the balloonists discovered a path leading off to the left, which could facilitate the deployment of Kent's division in that direction. Nevertheless, sending up the balloon was tactical folly. Pulled along by men holding guy wires, it provided the Spanish with a perfect indication of where Ameri-

can troops were moving. In addition, the balloon was an almost unmissable target, and Spanish fire sent it crashing to the ground. Fortunately the crew survived unharmed.

8-28 Brig. Gen. Samuel S. Sumner, commanding 1st Brigade, Wheeler's division

8-29 Signal Corps personnel inflate their observation balloon near El Pozo early on the morning of July 1.

8-30 The Signal Corps balloon rises from El Pozo.

The first of Wheeler's men to deploy were those of General Young's 2d Brigade, including the 10th Cavalry and the Rough Riders. Lieutenant Pershing and his 10th Cavalry reached the ford just in time to experience the truly devastating Spanish fire. His men "prepared for business" and stood in waist-high water awaiting the order to deploy. Spotting the Civil War veteran Wheeler on horseback in midstream, Pershing lifted his hat in salute. At that instant a Spanish shell fell between them, drenching both officers.

Few wartime experiences are said to be worse than being pinned down under accurate fire and unable to do anything about it, so the order to advance came as a relief, although deployment was slow. The Rough Riders had lost their colonel, not to the Spanish, but to promotion; however, the charismatic Roosevelt was well able to command (8-31). As they crossed the Aguadores River ford (8-32 and 8-33), they were positioned directly in front of Kettle Hill, somewhat to the west of San Juan Hill. At least one supply wagon overturned (8-34) as a result of hurrying over rough terrain.

While the cavalry under Sumner was moving on Kettle Hill, Kent (8-35), in command of the 1st Infantry Division, led his men toward San Juan

8-31 The Rough Riders' colonels—Col. Leonard Wood and Lt. Col. Theodore Roosevelt—seen here in Tampa, June 1898, with General Wheeler

8-32 A flood of troopers from the 1st Volunteer Cavalry, the Rough Riders, splash through the ford across the Aguadores River.

8-33 The Rough Riders move to the front across the Aguadores River.

8-34 In the rush to move supplies to the front, a transport wagon overturns in one of the streams near San Juan Hill

8-35 Brig. Gen. Jacob F. Kent, commanding the 1st Division. His men were to face the brunt of the fighting on San Juan Heights.

Heights. Commanding Kent's lead brigade was Brig. Gen. Hamilton S. Hawkins (8-36), who moved forward on the main road with the 6th and 16th Infantry (two-thirds of his brigade, less the 71st New York (8-37). Hawkins crossed the Aguadores River (8-38), moved left, went into line in a triangular piece of ground formed by the junction of the Aguadores and San Juan Rivers, and waited for

8-36 Brig. Gen. Hamilton S. Hawkins, commander of the lead brigade in Kent's division

8-37 Men of the 71st New York await orders to press forward toward the heights.

8-38 Moving forward on the main road leading to Santiago, men of Col. H. A. Theaker's 16th Infantry Regiment, Hawkins's brigade, cross the Aguadores River.

8-39 The trail left of the main road, discovered by the Signal Corps balloon, on which the 71st New York lay paralyzed and over which Kent's division advanced

the balance of the division (Col. Charles A. Wikoff and Col. E. P. Pearson's brigades, led by the 71st New York from Hawkins's brigade) to deploy on his left (8-39), taking the trail discovered by the Signal Corps balloon.

Though taking the lead, the New York Volunteers did not perform as well as the dismounted cavalry had so stoically at the river crossing farther north. As Pershing noted, the 71st "became demoralized and well-nigh stampeded . . . " under fire, with the lead battalion recoiling in disorder on the rear of the regiment. They had to be ordered to lie down to let Wikoff's men force their way through. There was some excuse for the panic of these green troops. Retreat was impossible, the road was clogged with men, and if they stayed in position, the deadly Spanish fire would decimate them. The Americans had little alternative but to advance across the river, which they did.

Colonel Wikoff (8-40), commanding the 3d Brigade, 1st Division, led the 13th Infantry across the river into an open space (8-41). A bullet struck

8-40 Col. Charles A. Wikoff, commanding the 3d Brigade, 1st Division, shown here as a field officer in the 19th Infantry

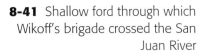

8-41 Shallow ford through which Wikoff's brigade crossed the San Juan River

8-42 Lt. Col. William S. Worth, commanding the 13th Infantry, Wikoff's brigade

8-43 Lt. Col. Emerson H. Liscum, commanding the 24th Infantry, Wikoff's brigade

8-44 Lt. Col. Ezra P. Ewers, commanding the 9th Infantry, Wikoff's brigade, shown here as a brigadier general

him and he died in minutes. Lt. Col. William S. Worth (8-42) of the 13th succeeded him. Within five minutes, he fell wounded. Lt. Col. Emerson H. Liscum (8-43) of the 24th took over, only to be badly wounded within the next five minutes. Then it was the turn of Lt. Col. Ezra P. Ewers (8-44) of the 9th Infantry regiment. The 3d Brigade had lost three different commanders in eleven minutes, although Ewers would survive the battle. His own 9th Infantry prepared to attack (8-45) from a fairly well-protected spot (8-46). Meanwhile Hawkins's

6th Infantry had taken a 25 percent loss in ten minutes and had to withdraw to reform.

Colonel Pearson's (8-47) 2d Brigade, 1st Division, followed Wikoff across the San Juan River and deployed on the far left flank of the American position. Another of his units, the 21st Infantry (8-48), and other U.S. regulars, were by that time pouring across the river (8-49).

Sumner, however, was taking heavy casualties while waiting to attack. He requested and received permission from Shafter to advance without coor-

8-45 Lt. Col. Ezra P. Ewers's 9th Infantry Regiment, Wikoff's brigade, prepares for the attack on San Juan Heights

8-46 Formed in the relative sanctuary of a tree line and sunken road along the San Juan River, men of the 9th Infantry await orders to attack.

8-47 Col. E. P. Pearson, commanding the 2d Brigade, 1st Division, shown here as commanding officer of the 10th Infantry

8-48 Crossing point of the 21st Infantry (Pearson's brigade) over the San Juan River

8-49 U.S. regulars cross the San Juan River

dinating with Kent. Then he sent his division forward up a small hill east of the ridge of San Juan Heights proper. Although the 1st Brigade was supposed to make the attack supported by the 2d, regiments in the 2d Brigade overtook the slower units of the 1st, mixing the two commands. All then quickened their pace, pushed their way through entanglements, and crossed the San Juan River.

Legend has it that Roosevelt led the charge up Kettle Hill, but actually the 9th Cavalry, an African-American unit, was in the van (8-50). Other units involved were the 1st Cavalry, part of the 10th Cavalry, and the Rough Riders. The Spanish fled before the Americans reached the summit, streaming back to the northern end of San Juan Heights. The American 3d and 6th and the remainder of the 10th Cavalry deflected to the left, joining Hawkins's right.

At the top of the hill the men found a number of huge iron kettles, probably used in sugar refining, which caused Roosevelt to name the hill just east of San Juan Heights "Kettle Hill" (8-51).

Having helped take the height and rout the Spanish, the Rough Riders had the unhappy task of seeking out their dead and wounded (8-52). Thankful to have survived, Roosevelt and his men

8-50 A painting depicting Troop C, 9th U.S. Cavalry, an African-American unit, leading the charge toward the summit of Kettle Hill

8-51 One of the kettles on "little San Juan Hill"

8-52 The Rough Riders search for dead and wounded comrades following the charge on Kettle Hill.

later posed for a photographer on San Juan Heights (8-53), in commemoration of the American sacrifice on Kettle Hill.

Any movement of Wheeler's cavalry forward to San Juan Heights would be partially blocked by a pond that was between Kettle and San Juan Hills (8-54). The cavalry would include the veterans of Kettle Hill, Roosevelt having received permission to attack San Juan Hill following the taking of Kettle Hill.

Meanwhile, farther south, Hawkins desperately endeavored to move his command forward to-

ward the heights. At 1:00 P.M., as the Gatling guns opened from the American lines, Hawkins sensed an opportunity and once again led his brigade forward across the San Juan River, this time joined by Ewers on the left and the cavalry on the right, which had detoured the fight on Kettle Hill. When his men faltered, Hawkins went to the front, screaming, "Come on, come on!" (8-55). With sword and hat raised, Lt. Jules G. Ord (8-56) likewise inspired his troops.

The charge was not a swift, spectacular, and orderly advance. The men went forward and up as

8-53 Lieutenant Colonel Roosevelt and his men on the heights overlooking Santiago

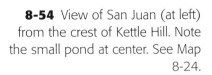

8-54 View of San Juan (at left) from the crest of Kettle Hill. Note the small pond at center. See Map 8-24.

8-55 Artist's rendition of General Hawkins exhorting his brigade toward the summit of San Juan Hill. With sword and hat raised, Lt. Jules Ord likewise inspires the troops at far right.

8-56 Lt. Jules Garesche Ord, 1st Brigade Commissary Officer, and hero of San Juan Hill

best they could, "moving slowly, carefully, with strenuous effort," as Richard Harding Davis described the scene. To Davis, that slow, stubborn tramping was "much more wonderful than any swinging charge could have been." "It was the best moment of anybody's life," wrote Stephen Crane. But the ever-present foreign observers were appalled. These men could not possibly take the blockhouse; it was "slaughter."

Hawkins was mortally wounded; Ord was killed as he leaped over the Spanish trench. As Hawkins's line advanced, Sumner's men (8-57), the Gatlings near the San Juan River ford (8-58), and several artillery batteries concentrated their fire into the Spanish trenches on the heights. At 1:30 P.M., the Americans swept onto the crest of the heights, firing on the retreating Spaniards as they fled.

Just as Hawkins, Ewers, and the cavalry reached the heights, the troops who had taken Kettle Hill rushed forward in the face of a destructive fire and pushed the Spanish off the northern portion of the heights back to their second line, some 600 to 800 yards to the rear. Simultaneously,

8-57 Painting by C. D. Graves depicting the advance on San Juan Hill

8-58 San Juan Hill as seen from the lower ford across the San Juan River

8-59 U.S. regulars struggle toward the blockhouse atop San Juan Hill in this artist's rendering.

8-60 Their brigade under the temporary command of Lieutenant Colonel Ewers, men of the 13th Infantry charge the blockhouse on San Juan Hill.

Pearson's brigade on the left wing performed a near-identical feat and captured the heights just south of San Juan Hill.

U.S. regulars moved against the blockhouse atop San Juan Hill, facing heavy fire (8-59), and men of the 13th Infantry charged and took it (8-60). Photograph 8-60 allegedly was taken during the battle, but close examination of the print in the National Archives shows that an artist added or touched up at least a portion of the tiny charging figures. Photograph 8-61 shows the blockhouse. Some veterans of San Juan Hill, such as Roosevelt, recalled the experience as exhilarating (8-62), but all too many needed prompt medical attention (8-63), and others were beyond it.

The wounded suffered considerably in the field hospitals (8-64). Many had to lie in the open, and the springless army wagons that transported the men back to El Pozo and then to the main hospital in Siboney jolted fearfully on the rutted roads. However wretched the circumstances, there had been improvements since the U.S. Civil War. Antiseptic measures and the cleaner nature of bullet wounds as compared to those of the American Civil War reduced the mortality rate from combat considerably compared to that of previous wars.

George Kennan of the Red Cross found the main hospital at Siboney fairly satisfactory, but the field hospital near the Aguadores River was in terrible shape. From Shafter's headquarters Kennan

8-62 Confident and proud, an American soldier stands guard with his regimental colors following the successful assault on San Juan Heights.

8-61 The blockhouse of San Juan Hill captured by the 13th Infantry

8-63 An ambulance at the foot of San Juan Hill awaits the arrival of casualties to be borne to the rear.

8-64 The 1st Division field hospital situated near the Aguadores River

phoned Clara Barton with a long list of necessities. Less than twenty-four hours later, "she rode into the hospital camp in an army wagon" loaded with supplies. Thenceforth the patients there did not lack for food and drink.

Incredibly, late in the afternoon of July 1, outnumbered ten to one, the Spanish counterattacked, but were driven back (8-65). Fighting continued between the two lines after dark and well into the next day (8-66), when Linares was

8-65 Spanish trenchline on San Juan Hill

8-66 East slope of San Juan Hill on July 2, one day after the battle

wounded. By noon of July 2, all of Lawton's division, having finally finished their work at El Caney at about 5:00 P.M. the previous afternoon, took a position on the far right flank of the army.

At 10:00 A.M. on July 3, Shafter sent forward a white flag, demanding a surrender. Negotiations commenced that brought an end to the major actions and initiated the Siege of Santiago.

El Caney and San Juan Heights had given the Americans increased respect for their Spanish opponents (8-67 and 8-68), who had fought hard and exacted a heavy payment in American lives.

Another group had also gained respect. It was a frankly racist age, and the Americans did not expect much from the African-American troops. But in the confusion of battle, units had intermingled, and the white soldiers saw for themselves how well their black comrades performed. Young Frank Knox, future secretary of the navy, became separated from the Rough Riders and

8-67 Wounded and forlorn, Spanish prisoners rest in the late afternoon shade following the American capture of the heights overlooking Santiago.

temporarily joined the 10th Cavalry. He wrote home, ". . . I must say that I never saw braver men anywhere. . . ." (8-69).

American losses for the three engagements totaled 205 killed and 1,180 wounded, a total that shocked Shafter (8-70 and 8-71). Spanish losses added up to 215 killed, 376 wounded, and 2 cap-

tured. These were severe losses, but there was not time to mourn or to reflect, because large events were pending—some expected, some unexpected. The American success had placed Admiral Cervera's becalmed squadron in a perilous situation. Would it sortie and fight, or stay and risk destruction in the harbor?

8-68 Lightly guarded by their captor, Spanish prisoners of war move glumly to the rear.

8-69 Triumphant African-American troops, possibly of the 10th Cavalry, pose after the battle.

8-70 A single headboard serves as a marker for four Americans of the 21st Infantry buried in the Spanish trenchline for which they fought on July 1, 1898.

8-71 A bit more care appears to have been given to the markers for these soldiers, who likewise lie buried in a trench.

CHAPTER 9

The Sea Battle of Santiago

To the sailors of the naval blockading squadron, the land action near Santiago, although admirable, seemed inconclusive. There could be no real victory while the Spanish squadron remained afloat. To be sure, it was relatively harmless as long as it remained in the harbor, but it was almost certain to sortie eventually. Initially, there had been doubts as to exactly what ships had even reached Santiago. Consequently, Lt. Victor Blue (9-1) of the armed lighthouse tender *Suwanee* had twice reconnoitered Santiago to determine the identity of Admiral Cervera's ships.

The Spanish squadron was still there, but Cervera had sent almost two-thirds of his men ashore to help defend the city. He knew that his ships were in no condition to face Admiral Sampson's, even if they were able to slip out of the harbor. There was no facility for drydocking his ships and overhauling them, so the hulls remained foul, reducing their speed significantly.

Safe in Spain, the ministry of marine urged Cervera on June 23 to clear the harbor as soon as possible. The next day, Cervera conferred with his captains; all agreed that this would be too dangerous. In fact, Cervera wrote pessimistically to Brigadier General Linares on June 25: "I have considered the squadron lost ever since it left Cape Verde, for to think anything else seems madness to me in view of the enormous disparity which exists between our own forces and those of the enemy."

On July 2, Gov. Gen. Ramón Blanco settled the matter, ordering Cervera to take his ships out as soon as possible. The admiral recalled his men from shore duty, but rather than leave that night, he decided to wait until morning. At night, the Americans played a powerful searchlight over the entrance and moved their ships in close.

The morning of Sunday, July 3, 1898, could not have been more beautiful. Capt. Robley D. Evans (9-2), skipper of the battleship *Iowa* (9-3), had just finished breakfast and was in his cabin chatting with his son, Naval Cadet Frank T. Evans, when at precisely 9:30 A.M. the general alarm sounded. The younger Evans exclaimed, "Papa, the enemy's ships are coming out!"

Cervera's plan—or rather, his forlorn hope—was to engage in a race rather than a battle. The squadron's orders were to head for Cienfuegos as rapidly as possible. Naval tacticians have second-guessed Cervera for the past century: he should have waited for overcast weather; he should have sent his ships in different directions. Probably neither of these alternatives would have helped the Spanish appreciably. The imminent fall of Santiago left the admiral few choices, none of them pleasant. He could take no action, and sur-

9-1 Lt. Victor Blue of the armed lighthouse tender *Suwanee*

9-2 Capt. Robley D. Evans, commanding officer of the battleship *Iowa*

9-3 *Iowa*, the newest battleship in the U.S. Navy

render his ships to the Americans and watch them be given American names and added to the U.S. Navy; he could scuttle the lot, a choice only marginally preferable; or he could take his chances, slim as they were, and at least meet defeat honorably at sea.

As if Fate wished to even the odds, however slightly, the U.S. squadron was not at full strength that morning. Admiral Sampson, its commander, was absent, the armored cruiser *New York* having left earlier that morning to take him to Siboney for a conference with General Shafter, taking with her the torpedo boat *Ericsson* and the armed yacht *Hist*. *Massachusetts*, *New Orleans*, and *Newark* lay at Guantánamo, coaling.

The ships that remained on station, however, were well able to handle the Spanish squadron, ranged in order east to west. First was the armed yacht *Gloucester*, which had started life as J. Pierpont Morgan's pleasure yacht *Corsair*. Next were the battleships *Indiana* (9-4), *Oregon* (9-5), and *Iowa*. *Texas* (9-6), which had been involved in so many accidents early in her career that she had

earned the nickname "The Old Hoodoo," was next. Then came the armored cruiser *Brooklyn* (9-7) and finally the armed yacht *Vixen* (9-8), which had been Philadelphia financier Peter Arrel Brown Widener's yacht *Josephine*. In the temporary absence of Admiral Sampson, Commodore Winfield Scott Schley (seen in 9-9 as a rear admiral) was the senior officer present afloat.

Although not at full strength, the Americans were on the alert, keeping the entrance to Santiago Bay (9-10) under constant observation. No sooner had Cervera's flagship, *Infanta María Teresa* (9-11) left the channel than the U.S. ships resounded with the alert that had electrified Captain Evans and his son. *Infanta María Teresa*'s sister ship, *Vizcaya*, followed the flagship. Then came what was probably Cervera's best ship, *Cristóbal Colón*, and after her *Almirante Oquendo*. Bringing up the rear were the torpedo boat destroyers *Plutón* and *Furor*.

Recognizing that battle could not be avoided, Capt. Victor María Concas y Palau (9-12), in command of *Infanta María Teresa*, and Cervera's new

9-4 *Indiana* at sea on the blockade, awnings and wind sails prominent because of the lack of ventilation in ships of that era

9-5 The battleship *Oregon*

9-6 The battleship *Texas* in Cuban waters, 1898

9-7 The armored cruiser *Brooklyn*

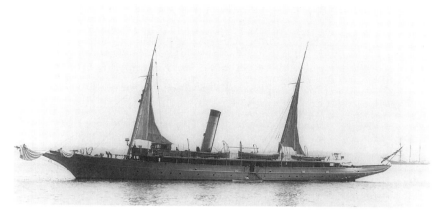

9-8 The armed yacht *Vixen*

9-9 Rear Admiral Winfield Scott Schley, photographed circa 1899. He commanded the Flying Squadron at Santiago.

9-10 Entrance to Santiago harbor, Cuba; El Morro at right

9-11 Admiral Cervera's flagship, the armored cruiser *Infanta María Teresa*—seen here at Saint Vincent, Cape Verde Islands, circa late April 1898—led the Spanish squadron out of Santiago Bay.

9-12 Captain Victor María Concas y Palau, commanding officer of *Infanta María Teresa*, became Admiral Cervera's chief of staff after Capt. Bustamente was mortally wounded on July 1.

chief of staff, ordered bugles blown to signal the beginning of action. "The sound of my bugles," Concas later observed sorrowfully, " . . . was the signal that the history of four centuries of grandeur was at an end and that Spain was becoming a nation of the fourth class." Turning to his "noble and beloved admiral," he lamented, "Poor Spain!"

The Spanish squadron managed to leave the harbor, turned starboard, and steamed west along the coast. *Brooklyn*, with Schley on board, altered course to follow. Capt. Francis A. Cook, *Brooklyn*'s skipper (9-13), ordered a 360-degree turn to avoid being rammed by *Infanta María Teresa* and to enable *Brooklyn* to pursue the enemy. It was a controversial move, although Schley later testified, "I should have done it in a second." The move took *Brooklyn* into the path of *Texas*. Schley claimed that *Texas* was never within six hundred yards of

the cruiser, and that the battleship "never entered my head as a menace or danger," but to the skipper of *Texas*, Capt. John W. Philip (9-14), a collision loomed. Philip ordered, "Back both engines hard!" *Brooklyn* passed harmlessly, and what had been potentially the most dangerous moment of the battle for the American forces had passed. *Brooklyn* and *Texas* are featured in a painting of the early stages of the battle (9-15).

The Americans concentrated their fire on the Spanish flagship. The first shot to strike cut an auxiliary steam pipe. Another exploded in Cervera's cabin and set the stern of the ship on fire. The latter underlined one of the major weaknesses of the Spanish ships: their wooden decks and much internal woodwork made them potential firetraps. A shell from Capt. Henry C. Taylor's (9-16) *Indiana* killed at least sixty men. Soon it became apparent

9-13 Capt. Francis A. Cook, commanding officer of the armored cruiser *Brooklyn*, leans against his ship's after 8-inch turret. Note the auxiliary steering position in left background.

9-15 In 1899, Alonzo Saenz, a Spanish navy surgeon and artist, depicted the Battle of Santiago, showing the emerging Spanish fleet engaging the armored cruiser *Brooklyn* (center) and the battleships *Iowa* and *Texas* (right).

9-14 Capt. John W. Philip, commanding officer of the battleship *Texas*

9-16 Capt. Henry C. Taylor, commanding officer of battleship *Indiana*.

that nothing but additional loss of life would result from further action and Cervera, who had taken command of his flagship after Concas had fallen wounded, decided to beach *Infanta María Teresa* (9-17). Cervera was the last man to leave the ship, reaching safety with the aid of his son, a lieutenant. Photograph 9-18 shows *Infanta María Teresa*'s after 11-inch turret.

Almirante Oquendo (9-19) was the next to come under heavy fire. The ship took about fifty hits, one of which exploded between the gun shield and gun of the forward turret (9-20), killing the turret captain, Lt. Eugenio Barcena, and all but one of the mount's crew. The ship, beyond saving, was run aground in flames.

This was the occasion of a cherished navy incident. As the tars on board *Texas* cheered in exultation and relief, Captain Philip is said to have admonished them, "Don't cheer, men; those poor fellows are dying." Capt. Juan B. Lazaga (9-21), *Almirante Oquendo*'s skipper, suffered a fatal heart attack as he was about to abandon ship.

Next to go were the two torpedo boat destroyers, under the command of Capt. Fernando

9-17 *Infanta María Teresa* aground off the coast of Cuba

9-18 *Infanta María Teresa*'s after 11-inch turret

9-19 The armored cruiser *Almirante Oquendo* at Saint Vincent, Cape Verde Islands, circa late April 1898

9-20 Forward turret and wrecked bridge of the armored cruiser *Almirante Oquendo*

9-21 Capt. Juan B. Lazaga, commanding officer of *Almirante Oquendo*

Villaamil (9-22), an officer "of great repute and noble lineage." These ships were small (9-23), but *Furor*, commanded by Lt. Cmdr. Diego Carlier (9-24), and *Plutón*, under the command of Lt. Cmdr. Pedro Vasquez (9-25), posed potential danger if they came near enough to an American ship to fire their torpedoes (9-26).

The task of intercepting them fell to *Gloucester*, under Cmdr. Richard Wainwright (9-27), who had been executive officer of *Maine* when she blew up. Despite the odds, he rushed his ship forward at full speed (9-28). *Vixen*, under Lt. Alexander Sharp (9-29), also engaged, and soon *Indiana, Iowa,* and *Oregon* joined, making this an exceedingly uneven contest. After the battle, Wainwright was a popular hero in the United States, where the idea of an armed yacht sinking two torpedo boat destroyers had great appeal. It is likely, however, that battleship fire finished off *Plutón*, which ran aground and blew up. *Furor* took a terrific beating from *Gloucester*'s guns, blew up, and sank. Captain Villaamil died of his wounds after reaching shore.

Only two Spanish ships, *Vizcaya* and *Cristóbal Colón* (9-30), remained afloat at that point. *Brooklyn, Iowa,* and *Texas* all set upon *Vizcaya*. Her skipper, Capt. Antonio Eulate (9-31), fought his ship

gallantly, and for a few minutes Schley, standing beside *Brooklyn*'s conning tower, thought *Vizcaya* might be pulling away. Chief Yeoman George Ellis (9-32) stood nearby, and Schley ordered him to check *Vizcaya*'s range. As Ellis began taking the range with a stadimeter, a shell from *Vizcaya* beheaded him. His was the only death the United States suffered in this sea battle.

Vizcaya, however, was too damaged to evade her pursuers (9-33). *Oregon* was particularly qualified for pursuit because her skipper, Capt. Charles E. Clark (9-34), had kept steam up in all of the ship's boilers. *Vizcaya* had been flying a beautiful silk flag, made and embroidered "by ladies of the province of Vizcaya," who had presented it to the ship. Knowing that his ship was doomed, Eulate ordered it lowered and burned and another less symbolic one hoisted. *Vizcaya*'s best efforts were in vain. On fire from many hits, the ship ran ashore some eighteen miles from the entrance to Santiago Bay.

The torpedo boat *Ericsson* and the armed yacht *Hist*, which had been accompanying *New York* when action was joined, were dispatched to rescue survivors (9-35). Lt. (j.g.) Felix M. Hunicke of *Hist*, who took photograph 9-35, was in charge

9-22 Capt. Fernando Villaamil, commanding the Spanish torpedo boat squadron; killed in action at Santiago

9-23 A *Terror*-class torpedo boat destroyer (either *Terror, Plutón,* or *Furor*) probably in the Cape Verde Islands, while en route to Cuba in April 1898

9-24 Lt. Cmdr. Diego Carlier, commanding officer of *Furor*

9-25 Lt. Cmdr. Pedro Vasquez, commanding officer of *Plutón*

9-26 Artist's depiction of Spanish torpedo boat destroyer (*Plutón* or *Furor*) attempting to run a withering gauntlet of American gunfire off Santiago

9-27 Cmdr. Richard Wainwright, commanding officer of *Gloucester*

9-28 Painting of the armed yacht *Gloucester* gallantly standing toward the emerging Spanish fleet off Santiago. She engaged *Plutón* and *Furor* and administered the coup de grace to both.

9-30 The Spanish armored cruisers *Cristóbal Colón* (left) and *Vizcaya* (right), anchored at Saint Vincent, Cape Verde Islands, en route to Cuba in April 1898

9-29 Lt. Alexander Sharp, commanding officer of the armed yacht *Vixen*

9-31 Capt. Antonio Eulate, commanding officer of *Vizcaya*

9-32 *Brooklyn's* Chief Yeoman George H. Ellis, circa 1898, the only American fatality at Santiago

9-33 Artist F. Bruno's rendition of the battleship *Oregon* (foreground) and the armored cruiser *Brooklyn* pursuing the Spanish armored cruiser *Vizcaya*.

9-34 Capt. Charles E. Clark, commanding officer of the battleship *Oregon*

9-35 The grounded Spanish cruiser *Vizcaya* burns on the coast of Cuba after the Battle of Santiago, as photographed by Lt. (j.g.) Hunicke of *Hist*. The torpedo boat destroyer *Ericsson* stands by at right. In the foreground is *Hist*'s first cutter, standing toward the wrecked ship.

of one of the boats as it rescued *Vizcaya*'s survivors while she lay burning and exploding. *Iowa* left the action to engage in this work of mercy, sending boats to the rescue and receiving the prisoners (9-36). Many of *Vizcaya*'s survivors were in a dangerous situation, having taken refuge on a sandspit between the burning ship and the beach. Sharks menaced them from the sea and Cuban insurgents from the shore. Other survivors were still on board *Vizcaya*, threatened by the rapidly spreading fire, which had burned out by the time photographs 9-37, 9-38 and 9-39 were taken.

Those picked up by the small craft were taken to *Iowa*. Learning that Captain Eulate was among them, Evans prepared to receive his fellow officer with appropriate honors. As the boat carrying Eulate and a few others neared the ship, Evans saw that the Spanish captain had been wounded and ordered a chair lowered. As Eulate came over the side, *Iowa*'s guard "presented arms, the officer of the deck saluted, and the Spanish prisoners already on board stood at attention."

Eulate slowly rose, removed his sword belt, and after reverently kissing the sword's hilt, offered his sword to Evans. The American officer grasped Eulate's hand, however, and said, "Keep your sword, sir. You have fought like a brave and gallant sailor." Those of *Iowa*'s crew who witnessed this exchange burst into cheers, a spontaneous action that deeply moved Eulate, who later stated, "It was

9-36 Artist's conception of boats from *Iowa* coming to rescue *Vizcaya*'s crew as the stricken Spanish ship lies aground on Acerraderos Reef

9-37 The wrecked Spanish cruiser *Vizcaya*. Note the extensive fire damage. Her fallen mainmast lies across the 11-inch turret.

9-38 *Vizcaya*'s after 11-inch turret, whose gunners gallantly battled *Iowa* and *New York* at one point in the battle. The size of the man standing atop the mount serves as a useful yardstick to gauge its size. Her fallen mainmast lies at left.

9-39 Starboard side of *Vizcaya*'s spar deck, showing how wooden planking has been entirely burned away; note the shielded 5.5-inch gun at right

the proudest moment of my life." As Evans led him to the cabin where his wounds would be treated, Eulate "turned toward his ship, and stretching up his right hand, exclaimed, '¡Adiós *Vizcaya*!'" At that precise moment the ship's forward magazine exploded (9-40).

Only one Spanish man-of-war remained in action, and that was the *Cristóbal Colón*. This armored cruiser had certain advantages. Built for speed, technically she had the capability of outpacing any American ship present, and her commanding officer, Capt. Emilio Díaz Moreu (9-41), was said to have been by far the ablest officer in the fleet. *Cristóbal Colón* also had serious disadvantages, however; her main battery had not been fitted (9-42) and her crew was inexperienced.

When *Vizcaya* had been disposed of, *Cristóbal Colón* had a six-mile advantage, and an all-out chase began. With the end of the battle in sight and having suffered so little in casualties and damage, the American officers and men apparently took this final action in the spirit of a glorified boat race. A photographer on board the *Oregon* wandered about snapping pictures.. A young naval cadet standing near Captain Clark would become Fleet Admiral William D. Leahy.

9-40 Magazine explosion wrecks the doomed *Vizcaya*.

9-41 Capt. Emilio Díaz Moreu, commanding officer of *Cristóbal Colón*

9-42 Captain Moreu and officers of the armored cruiser *Cristóbal Colón*. Note empty gun mount behind them.

Photograph 9-43 shows Clark with a number of his officers and men.

Those for whom the chase was no pleasure jaunt were the sweating sailors in the machinery spaces, straining to maintain their ships at top speed in the suffocating heat. On board *Brooklyn* Schley thought of them with sympathetic admiration. This being the pre–Josephus Daniels navy, *Brooklyn* carried a supply of cool beer, earmarked for the officers. Organizing a virtual bucket brigade of sailors, Schley had the beverage sent down to these invaluable heroes. Moreover, he stationed an ensign to report down to them the progress of the action.

For a while it seemed that *Cristóbal Colón* would escape. Then, slowly, the tiny image of the fleeing ship grew larger as the Americans gradually closed the distance. *Cristóbal Colón* had used up all her best coal, and the inferior stuff remaining could not generate sufficient steam. The pursuers gradually pulled within range (9-44). Moreu struck his colors at 1:15 P.M. and ran his ship aground some fifty miles west of Santiago. As a result of this early surrender, *Cristóbal Colón* suffered by far the least of any Spanish ship as far as the human toll was concerned—one killed and sixteen wounded.

Moreu based his action on common sense rather than cowardice. The Americans had already won the battle of Santiago so decisively that no action his ship might take could affect the issue. Further resistance would result only in need-

9-43 Capt. Charles E. Clark (with binoculars), *Oregon*'s captain, joins Lts. Albert A. Ackerman (in charge of the after 13-inch turret) and Reginald F. Nicholson (*Oregon*'s navigator), Ens. Charles L. Hussey, Naval Cadets Paul B. Dungan and Edward C. Kalbfus, and Marine orderlies, Pvts. Charles H. Haight and Ferdinand F. Ellis on the roof of *Oregon*'s after 13-inch turret during the Battle of Santiago. Also present are Gunner's Mate First Class James F. Groves, Seaman Johan E. Nord, and Apprentices Second Class Benjamin B. Wood and George C. Love.

9-44 Lt. Cmdr. James K. Cogswell, *Oregon*'s executive officer; behind him, signalmen "wig-wag" to the armored cruiser *Brooklyn* "Your shots are falling short" during the chase of the Spanish cruiser *Cristóbal Colón*.

less casualties. Moreu, however, did attempt to keep his ship from becoming an American prize, for at the moment of surrender or shortly thereafter, he ordered her seacocks opened. If it had been after the surrender, as some Americans assumed at the time, this action was contrary to the laws of war, and it aroused considerable indignation. To do Moreu justice, it is highly probable that he gave the order shortly before striking the colors, and in the confusion of the moment action was delayed. However incongruous such niceties may appear to the layman, they were taken very seriously by those who followed the profession of arms at sea.

Oregon's crew erupted in cheers when the Spanish flag descended, and *Oregon*'s bugle blew "cease firing" (9-45). On board *Texas*, Captain Philip once again stopped the cheering and led his men to the quarterdeck, where he offered a prayer of thanksgiving "for the almost bloodless victory." After listening in reverent silence, hats off, his crew gave their captain a hearty cheer.

Schley sent word by Captain Cook, his chief of staff and *Brooklyn*'s commanding officer, that the Spanish officers could keep their personal effects. *Oregon* dispatched a prize crew to take over *Cristóbal Colón* (9-46), whose officers waited on her quarterdeck to be taken to the transport *Resolute* (9-47). The Spanish ship later capsized as *New York* attempted to ease her into shallow water (9-48).

When the firing began, Rear Admiral Sampson, Capt. French E. Chadwick (9-49) of *New York*, and his officers and crew could hear the sounds of battle and immediately changed course back to Santiago; however, the flagship did not arrive in time to participate in the action. No doubt Sampson was frustrated and irascible; of all times to be away from his post—on the very morning the Spanish sortied! In addition, he was not fond of Schley, so Schley's exultant message, "A glorious victory has been achieved. Details follow," may well have galled him. There was really no excuse for not acknowledging it, for sending no word of congratulations to his valiant men, if not to Schley personally. The latter tried again: "This is a great day for our country." This drew a curt "Report casualties" (9-50). Schley repeated the words as if he could not believe them and walked away.

9-45 Reflecting the "most intense enthusiasm" prevailing on board, *Oregon*'s crew cheers as the *Cristóbal Colón* strikes her colors at 1:15 P.M. on July 3.

9-46 Prize crew from the battleship *Oregon*, under Lt. Cmdr. James K. Cogswell, rows toward the surrendered *Cristóbal Colón*.

9-47 Spanish officers on *Cristóbal Colón*'s quarterdeck await transportation to the transport *Resolute*.

9-48 The Spanish armored cruiser *Cristóbal Colón* lies on her beam ends in the surf off the mouth of the Tarquino River.

9-49 Capt. French E. Chadwick, commanding officer of the armored cruiser *New York*

Much work remained for the American officers and crews, who were required to report on the condition of the Spanish ships (9-51 and 9-52). Another victim would be added the next day, when the Spanish attempted to sink the cruiser *Reina Mercedes* in the channel (9-53). Fire from *Massachusetts* and *Texas* hastened the process. The next year the Americans refloated *Reina Mercedes* and towed her to the United States.

The main task at the moment, however, lay in picking up survivors and rescuing the wounded. Captain Cook had ordered his men to show no sign of triumph as they rowed up to *Cristóbal Colón*. Evidently the Spanish sailors appreciated the sportsmanship, greeting them with shouts of "¡*Bravo Americanos*!" Not to be outdone, the men of *Brooklyn* responded "¡*Bravo Españoles*!"

Many of *Cristóbal Colón*'s crewmen were in bad shape. They had been among those sent ashore to help defend the city, and had not received food for thirty-six hours. Then they had embarked on their ships, only to find no food was ready for them. There was no shortage of brandy, however, and these half-starved men received large doses, with predictable results. As one officer reported, "One of the first duties of the prize crew was to break or throw overboard the half-emptied brandy bottles laying about the decks."

Rescuing those stranded in the ships that were more seriously battered than *Cristóbal Colón*

9-50 The flagship *New York*, her crew cheering *Oregon* after the conclusion of the Battle of Santiago, flies the signal 2F-94: "Report Casualties."

9-51 U.S. sailors poke around the topside wreckage on board *Almirante Oquendo*, probably on July 9, 1898. The inspecting Americans found the ship to be a "structural wreck . . . practically broken in two."

9-52 The Spanish cruiser *Almirante Oquendo* aground off the coast of Cuba. Note how graffiti artists have scrawled their initials for posterity on the after turret.

9-53 The Spanish cruiser *Reina Mercedes*, sunk near the channel to Santiago harbor, July 4, 1898, in an unsuccessful attempt to block the channel that reprised the Americans' efforts with collier *Merrimac* a month earlier.

posed a real danger. In fact, it is said that when Admiral Cervera was brought on board *Gloucester*, he urged that her men not be sent on board *Infanta María Teresa*'s burning hull, lest explosions kill the rescuers. American determination to rescue as many of the Spanish as possible from a horrible death on board the rapidly heating ships (9-54 and 9-55), however, matched Cervera's chivalrous concern.

Later Cervera was transferred to *Iowa*, where Captain Evans welcomed him with all due ceremony and genuine cordiality. "As the brave old admiral came over the side . . . ," Evans later recounted, "without shirt or hat, but an admiral every inch of him, the officers saluted and the marines presented arms, and the bugles sounded the salute for an officer of his rank."

The admiral appeared to be in good spirits and may well have been relieved, for the tragedy he had feared and expected had happened, taking with it the curse of an impossible responsibility. Indeed, several Spanish officers admitted feeling relief. One spoke of the nervous strain they had been under, knowing that they would be sailing to their destruction, but honor and duty left them no

9-54 The battleship *Texas* and a converted yacht—most likely *Hist*—stand by the grounded and armored Spanish cruisers *Almirante Oquendo* and *Infanta María Teresa*.

9-55 Smoke from the funeral pyres of the Spanish cruisers *Almirante Oquendo* (left) and *Infanta María Teresa* (right)

alternative. "There was no way out of it," he said, "and since it had to come, I cannot but feel relieved that it is over, and I am grateful to God that we have fallen into such kind hands." Not only the Spanish officers won admiration, however; an American officer expressed appreciation for the "patience and fortitude" of the wounded enlisted men, many of whom had suffered terrible injuries in the destruction of their ships.

Credit for the victory at Santiago, however, soon proved controversial. On the afternoon of July 3, Sampson sent a message to Washington, listing the results of the engagement. He began, "The fleet *under my command* offers the nation, as a Fourth of July present, the destruction of the whole of Cervera's fleet . . . " (italics added). This did not set well with those who viewed the ex-

pression "under my command" as a deliberate attempt to slight Schley.

Every Spanish ship was put out of action, at a cost to the United States of one man killed and one wounded. In contrast, the Spanish lost 323 dead, 151 wounded, and 1,720 taken prisoner. Yet this overwhelming victory revealed a major weakness, the assessment of which would result in improvements to the U.S. Navy a few years later. American marksmanship had been poor. Later, a board of inquiry found no more than 123 apparent hits out of 9,433 shots in the hulls of the four Spanish cruisers. Despite the need for improvement, however, the fact remained that Cervera's fleet had been destroyed, and with it Spain's hopes of maintaining its empire in the Western Hemisphere.

The Santiago Campaign—Part II

As dawn broke over Santiago de Cuba (10-1) on July 3, 1898, the American positions appeared quite formidable. On the right was Brig. Gen. Henry W. Lawton's 2d Division, consisting of the 1st, 2d, and 3d Brigades, under the commands of Brig. Gen. William Ludlow, Col. N. S. Miles, and Col. A. R. Chaffee, respectively. Also on the right was Wheeler's cavalry division, made up of the 1st, 9th, and 10th Cavalry and the Rough Riders. Brig. Gen. John C. Bates's Independent Brigade held the center, with Brig. Gen. Jacob F. Kent's 1st Division on the left.

On July 2, four batteries had been placed to bombard Santiago and a portion of its entrenchments so that Ludlow's force could cover the city from the north. Bombardment of the Spanish lines began early on the morning of July 3 (10-2). Key locations of American positions appear on map 10-3. The next twenty photographs (10-4 through 10-23) show the American positions,

10-1 Santiago seen from afar, viewed from an observation tower erected in the siege lines

10-2 Accompanied by his staff officers, Lt. Col. Ezra P. Ewers (left), temporary commander of Wikoff's 3d Brigade, 1st Division, watches the bombardment of the Spanish lines early on July 3.

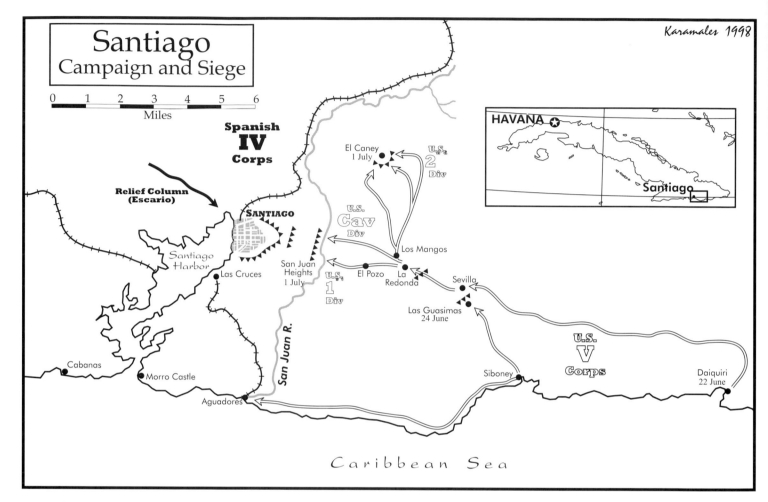

10-3 The siege of Santiago

from north to south and curving around the eastern side of Santiago. Photograph 10-4 shows Cuban troops under General Calixto García moving past the U.S. right flank toward their position in the siege lines northwest of Santiago. To the north of the city, the 4th Infantry was entrenched on a small hill west of the St. Iñez Road to Cuabitas and El Cristo (10-5).

Northeast of Santiago, flimsy shelters called "bombproofs" in the camps of the 7th and 12th Infantry straddled the St. Iñez Road (10-6). Along the same road, men of the 7th Infantry occupied trenches and rifle pits (10-7). North of the road leading to El Caney, the 71st New York Volunteers extended their lines (10-8). On the north side of San Juan Heights, the Rough Riders (10-9) extended their left flank north of the Santiago-Siboney road, where their lines met those of the

10th Cavalry. Ready for action, a trooper located on the 10th Cavalry's right flank aimed the much-heralded Sims-Dudley dynamite gun at the Spanish siege lines (10-10). Several Gatling guns lay along the American siege lines (10-11). Photograph 10-12 shows one of the machine guns in use on San Juan Hill. North of the blockhouse on San Juan Hill, 6th Cavalry troopers crouched in the front line of trenches to avoid sniper fire from the Spanish positions (10-13). From their trenches just north of the captured blockhouse on San Juan Hill, men of the 9th Infantry had a good view of Santiago (10-14). The regimental colors marked the center of the 9th Infantry's position (10-15). This and similar flags provided excellent targets for Spanish fire, but the Americans were immensely proud of their units and would have resisted strongly any suggestion that their colors be

10-4 Cuban troops move past the American right flank to take up their position.

10-5 North of Santiago, the 4th Infantry moves into position. This view looks southwest.

10-6 "Bombproofs" along the St. Iñez Road

10-7 Men of the 7th Infantry occupy trenches and rifle pits northeast of Santiago along the St. Iñez Road. This view looks northwest.

10-8 Looking southwest toward Santiago, the 71st New York Volunteers extend their lines.

taken down. Nor was this the only hazard. The reverse slope of San Juan Hill had been terraced to provide suitable campsites, which left the men stationed there exposed to Spanish mortar fire (10-16).

The headquarters of Colonel Ewers of the 9th Infantry was readily recognizable. Instead of a tent flap, it boasted the luxury of a thatched shelter (10-17). The 24th Infantry (10-18) was situated directly west of the blockhouse. On a hill in front

10-9 On their position on San Juan Heights, the Rough Riders of the 1st Volunteer Cavalry entrench their left flank.

10-10 A trooper trains the Sims-Dudley dynamite gun on the Spanish siege lines.

10-11 Troopers of the 10th Cavalry man one of several Gatling guns.

10-12 A Colt Automatic Gun in the trenches on San Juan Hill

10-13 6th Cavalry troopers crouch in a trench to avoid possible sniper fire.

10-14 Men of the 9th Infantry gaze on Santiago from the trenches just north of the captured blockhouse, in background. This view looks south.

10-15 Flying proudly in a hot, brisk Cuban breeze, regimental colors mark the centerline of the 9th Infantry's position on San Juan Hill.

10-16 Camps on the reverse slope of San Juan Hill were vulnerable to Spanish mortar fire.

10-17 Colonel Ewers's headquarters during the siege of Santiago. Note the thatched shelter erected in lieu of a tent fly.

10-18 This view from the 24th Infantry's position looks southwest.

of the 9th Infantry trenches, the men of the 21st Infantry had established their bombproofs (10-19) east of Santiago. The 2d Infantry (10-20) was part of the command of Col. E. P. Pearson, who led the 2d Brigade of the 1st Division. His headquarters were located on the road leading to Güines (10-21). Photographs 10-22 and 10-23 show the views looking south from the 2d Infantry's rifle pits and from the left wing of the V Corps lines, respectively.

On the night of July 2, Shafter held a council of war where, in the sedate words of a contemporary history, "misgivings were expressed." And well they might be. Both Major General Shafter and Major General Wheeler were ill with fever; Brig. Gen. S.B.M. Young, in command of Wheeler's second brigade, was so sick he had to be sent to the hospital ship. The men were suffering from heat and short rations. The army's failure to establish a

provision depot meant that usually no more than one day's rations were on hand at the front. And over all hung the threat of yellow fever, the dreaded "Yellow Jack." Correspondent Richard Harding Davis reported, "One smelt disaster in the air." His friend Theodore Roosevelt was equally pessimistic, informing Senator Henry Cabot Lodge, "We are on the brink of a terrible military disaster." He asked Lodge for reinforcements, artillery, ammunition, and especially food.

Early on July 3, Shafter wrote to Secretary of War Alger that the American line was thin and the Spanish defenses were strong, so he was considering withdrawing some five miles behind his current lines. Under these circumstances, Shafter's next action seemed remarkably like a bluff. At 8:30 A.M. he wrote to General José Toral, who had replaced Brigadier General Linares in command of Spanish forces at Santiago, "Sir: I shall be

10-19 Bombproofs of the 21st Infantry east of Santiago on a hill directly in front of the 9th Infantry trenches, looking north

10-20 A view of the 2d Infantry's trenches

obliged, unless you surrender, to shell Santiago de Cuba. Please inform the citizens of foreign countries and all women and children that they should leave the city before 10 o'clock tomorrow morning." In keeping with the custom of the time, he ended, "very respectfully, your obedient servant."

These events took place before the sea battle. The first report received stated that the Spanish had soundly defeated Sampson's squadron, and gloom seized the Americans. Then came word of the victory. Spirits soared as a regimental band played "The Star-Spangled Banner" and "There'll Be a Hot Time in the Old Town Tonight." Also heartening was a message from Alger, who instructed Shafter to hold his position and promised reinforcements, some of whom left Tampa that same day, July 3.

Meanwhile, Escario's relief column of some 3,500 men had reached Santiago. This was at best a mixed blessing, however; Toral could use the manpower, but it meant 3,500 more mouths to feed, and the city was already on the verge of starvation. Still, Toral had no authority to surrender even if he wished, only Madrid or the captain general in Havana could do so.

At about 6:30 P.M. he sent his reply to Shafter's ultimatum. The city would not surrender, and he would notify the foreign authorities. With the messenger came several consuls, who asked for more time to evacuate the fifteen thousand to twenty thousand noncombatants. Shafter granted the noncombatants permission to go to El Caney, but not to Siboney, lest the hospital there be infected with "Yellow Jack" and other diseases. He also granted a delay in the bombardment until noon on July 5.

Lieutenant Pershing noted that both sides were glad of the respite. Trooper Frank Knox wrote home rather wistfully, "Santiago is a pretty place. It seems a shame to lay it in ruins."

Evacuation began on July 4 and totaled about eighteen thousand. Among them were several high officials, who departed in defiance of General Toral's orders. They painted a grim picture of conditions in the city—Spanish losses were great, food was scarce, and the poor were starving. The

10-21 Headquarters tents of Col. E. P. Pearson, commanding the 2d Brigade of the 1st Division

10-22 View looking south down the line of rifle pits manned by the 2d Infantry

10-23 Palm trees mark the extreme left wing of the V Corps lines surrounding Santiago, looking south, probably through the lines of the 9th Massachusetts Volunteers.

people were eager to surrender. But most of the refugees were simply civilians caught in the machinery of war, and the small town of El Caney was ill equipped to handle them.

The next morning, Tuesday, July 5, Toral sent a messenger under a flag of truce. Instead of blindfolding him, as was the custom, in a canny bit of psychological warfare the Americans led him open-eyed past the batteries and lines. He asked for more time to communicate with Madrid and for the return of the British cable operators, who had left the city. Evidently, Toral had heard of the destruction of the Spanish fleet but could not believe it. Shafter's long reply left no illusions on that score. *St. Louis*, with Admiral Cervera aboard, had sailed for the United States. "Our fleet is now perfectly free to act." Unless the city surrendered by noon on July 9, bombardment would begin. Shafter assured the Spanish commander that he did not want to kill any more of Toral's men or his own.

During this and other truces the Americans did what they could to strengthen their positions. Trench lines were extended (10-24), artillery was

10-24 American forces extend their trench lines in front of Santiago during the steamy morning of July 7, 1898.

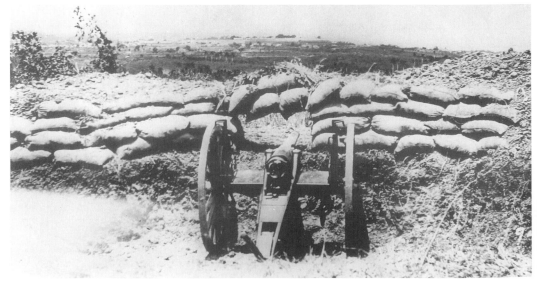

10-25 Behind a revetment of earth and sandbags, an American artillery piece is trained on Santiago.

positioned (10-25), and shelters were improvised to provide some relief from the relentless heat (10-26). Of course, there was no relief from the flood of paperwork (10-27).

Toral replied to Shafter with what in retrospect seems a very sensible counteroffer. His men would evacuate the city in exchange for safe passage to Holguín, retaining their equipment and weapons. Shafter found this reasonable, but when he forwarded the proposal to the War Department, he received a stern reply: "You will accept nothing but an unconditional surrender, and should take extra precautions to prevent the enemy's escape." Shafter countered, stressing the advantages. Loss of life would be avoided, the harbor was in American control, the refugees could return to their homes. What is more, three cases of yellow fever had been reported at Siboney. All the Americans had to lose were Spanish prisoners, whom they did not want.

But Washington would have no part of this realistic approach. Since the Civil War, "unconditional surrender" had become something of a mantra. Oddly enough, it was President McKinley, the erst-

10-26 Underneath a thatched shelter, officers of the 17th Infantry seek relief from the merciless heat.

10-27 Paperwork clutters the desk in the office of the 31st Michigan Volunteers' adjutant, temporarily taken over by the mustachioed regimental sergeant-major.

while dove, who dictated a stiff and indeed insulting reply: "The Secretary of War orders, when you are strong enough to destroy the enemy and take Santiago, that you do it." Thus irrevocably committed, Shafter's support force worked hard to ensure against any interruption in communications (10-28 and 10-29) and aerial reconnaissance (10-30 and 10-31).

Many under Shafter's command disapproved of his willingness to negotiate. In general, the enlisted men were impatient and would have preferred action to waiting about while the top brass discussed details. The ever-eager Roosevelt was scornful of Shafter's "tacking and veering," as he termed it when writing to Senator Lodge on July 10. He felt that it would be "a great misfortune to accept less than unconditional surrender." A few more days of fighting, "chiefly bombardment," should finish off "the whole Spanish army. . . ." At the same time, he hoped a direct assault on the city would not be necessary, for he feared this would cost a quarter of his men.

No one seems to have expressed the thought in writing, but behind the bombast one senses fear—a feeling that if they did not attack soon they would not be able to attack at all. The men were in bad shape. Food was scarce and poor, and what little they had the men were generously sharing with the pathetic refugees. Health was deteriorating rapidly. Some rudimentary precau-

tions were taken, such as boiling drinking water (10-32), but the obviously polluted pond near San Juan and Kettle Hills was not placed off limits, and the men swam in it freely (10-33). Malaria was rampant, and over all brooded the shadow of Yellow Jack. The wary glance this soldier casts at his regimental mascot, a golden eagle (10-34), might be considered symbolic of men ready, even eager, to fight, but wanting to get it over.

In accordance with his orders from Washington, Shafter advised Toral that he must either surrender or expect bombardment at 4:00 P.M. on July 10. Actually, it was somewhat after 5:00 P.M. that *Brooklyn*, *Texas*, and *Indiana* began bombarding, but their shells fell short. Field guns, mortars, Gatling guns, and the dynamite gun fired on Spanish defenses outside Santiago; however, no attempt was made to advance on the city. The Spanish responded, but not enthusiastically. A little fighting took place on the San Juan Heights, and the United States lost Capt. Charles W. Powell and one private killed, with four wounded.

On the next day, July 11, *New York* joined in shelling Santiago from 9:27 A.M to 1:00 P.M., with no better result than on the previous day. Also on July 11, Alger made a proposal that was sensible as well as humane: Spanish prisoners should not be brought to the United States but sent back to Spain at American expense. This would cost no more than establishing and maintaining prisoner

10-28 Signal Corps personnel prepare for construction of a telegraph line.

10-29 Lt. Col. O. Pierson, Officer in Charge of the Signal Corps Telegraph Office in Washington, D.C., seen against a background of document boxes

10-30 Signal Corps personnel and their aerial photographic equipment

10-31 A balloon carries an aerial camera skyward.

10-33 The pond at the foot of San Juan Hill and in front of Kettle Hill provided welcome refreshment for the troops camped nearby General Wheeler's headquarters. This view was from behind the position of the 6th Infantry on July 5.

10-32 American soldiers boil drinking water for their unit during the siege.

10-34 Pocatello Jo, an appropriate regimental mascot, rests on the outstretched arm of a wary soldier.

of war camps and was good psychology. Obviously, Alger expected Santiago to fall in the very near future.

At this time, Shafter's force numbered about 22,500, not counting the sick and wounded. Small groups of reinforcements began arriving. As they approached Santiago from Siboney or Daiquiri, they discovered that what they took at first to be broken fences were actually Spanish barbed-wire fences, which proved a formidable barrier. The strands had to be carefully clipped, and meanwhile the men were stuck in position, vulnerable to Spanish Mauser bullets.

On July 12, major reinforcements arrived. General Nelson A. Miles, the U.S. Army commander in chief, arrived with eight thousand men. The next day he, Shafter, and Toral met for ninety minutes. The U.S. position was unconditional surrender; Toral's was that he must defend the city unless otherwise ordered. Shafter extended the truce to July 14 to allow Toral time to contact his superiors.

In Havana, Blanco had been blustering that surrender was impossible, but the creoles were frankly hoping for an American victory and even the *peninsulares* were wavering. Linares, Toral's predecessor, was ill, but on July 12 he dictated a telegram to Madrid stating that surrender was inevitable and "we are only prolonging the agony."

Meanwhile, disease was riddling the American forces (10-35). Camp hospitals were established (10-36) and rapidly filled. The sick and wounded were evacuated to the mainland as soon as pos-

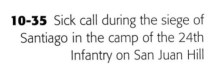
10-35 Sick call during the siege of Santiago in the camp of the 24th Infantry on San Juan Hill

10-36 Camp hospital behind the American siege lines

sible (10-37). One of the worst locations was Siboney, site of the main military hospital. Typhoid had been running rampant, and yellow fever broke out on July 11. Desperate and not knowing what else to do, the Americans burned the town on July 14 (10-38). A commission of the Medical Corps under Maj. Walter Reed (10-39) studied the origin and spread of typhoid fever through the camps and concluded that dust and unclean conditions helped spread the disease. A few years later, another Reed commission would prove that the *Aedes aegypti* mosquito spread yellow fever.

The hospital ship *Relief* (10-40) stood by off Siboney to receive casualties (10-41). She had been built between 1895 and 1896 as the steel passenger liner *John Englis*, and in 1898 the army

10-37 Sick and wounded soldiers await evacuation to the mainland, crowding a hospital tent at Siboney, one week after the Battle of San Juan Hill.

10-38 Americans burned disease-ridden Siboney on July 14, 1898.

10-39 Maj. Walter Reed, Medical Corps

10-40 The hospital ship *Relief* stands by off Siboney, ready to take casualties on board during the siege of Santiago.

10-41 Sailors prepare to transfer the sick and wounded to *Relief* during July 1898.

had acquired her for use as a hospital ship. Although she was a long way from satisfactory by today's standards, the patients probably found her berths welcome after the hospital tents (10-42), and the nurses in their cumbersome uniforms provided a glimpse of American womanhood (10-43). Not many years had passed since Florence Nightingale had made nursing a respectable profession, and these women were more or less pioneers. The doctors did the best they could with the existing equipment and under the prevailing conditions (10-44 and 10-45).

Ashore, the truce continued (10-46), but obviously matters were moving toward a climax. General Miles assumed command of the army in Cuba on July 13 (10-47). He and Shafter, with a few advisers, met that morning (10-48) to discuss the situation and, as a result, sent Toral another notification. Toral replied at once, requesting a personal meeting with Shafter. The conference took place under a cottonwood tree, 125 feet high and 10 feet in diameter, conveniently located between the two forces (10-49). Miles and Shafter were accompanied by a Colonel Maus and a Captain McKitrick,

10-42 Relief's Ward 3

10-43 Nurses serving on board *Relief*

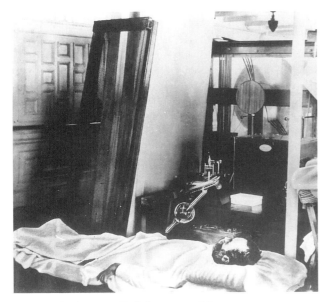

10-44 Patient on *Relief* prepared for an x-ray

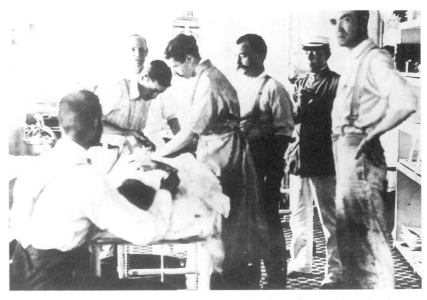

10-45 *Relief's* army surgeons operate under less than antiseptic circumstances.

with a Señor Mendoza as translator. Toral brought a Colonel Valesquez and the British vice consul at Santiago, Robert Mason, as interpreter.

For a while the discussion followed the usual course, Toral holding that his government would permit him to surrender the city but not his troops and Shafter demanding unconditional surrender. He pointed out the hopelessness of the Spanish position and reminded Toral that the Americans were capable of taking the city by assault. To this Toral is quoted as saying, "Even if that can be done, yet it is to be remembered that every soldier in my army is ready to die to maintain the honor of my country." To which Shafter retorted "that while it is honorable in his soldiers to be willing to die, it is a damned poor sort of honor in their

10-46 The truce is on. American volunteers set their Springfield rifles between sandbags and sit atop their earthworks.

10-47 General Miles, U.S. Army commander in chief, chats with an officer during the negotiations.

10-48 Generals Shafter (left) and Miles confer regarding the prospects of Spanish surrender. Shafter wears the distinctive model 1889 fatigue helmet, which became a personal trademark of the corps commander during the Santiago Campaign.

10-49 The "Surrender Tree" between the Spanish and American lines

country which requires them to die for no purpose. We call it murder."

Eventually, Toral admitted that his position was hopeless. He asked for and was granted certain concessions, largely symbolic. His troops would turn their arms and ammunition over to their own officers, Spanish officers could retain their side arms, and the troops would march out with military honors. The conferees agreed to appoint commissioners to draw up the agreement.

When word reached the American troops that, except for formalities, Santiago had surrendered, the men erupted in cheers, joyous laughter, and song. Someone started to sing a Christian hymn,

and the sound spread along miles of entrenchments.

The formal surrender took place on Sunday, July 17, under the cottonwood tree where Toral waited. At 9:00 A.M. all the American division and brigade commanders and their staffs met Shafter at his headquarters. The procession to the tree began with Shafter in the lead, Wheeler at his side, Lawton and Kent behind, and the rest according to rank, all accompanied by a detachment of the 2d Cavalry under Capt. Lloyd M. Brett.

As Shafter walked down the slope toward the tree, Toral advanced a bit and raised his hat, and Shafter returned the salute (10-50 and 10-51).

10-51 A photograph of the shaking of hands at the Surrender Tree, probably at leave-taking

10-50 An artist's rendering of the meeting between the American and Spanish generals on the morning of July 17, 1898. Here, General Toral extends a hand, presumably to General Shafter, although Miles is pictured at right.

10-52 Religious services on San Juan Hill after the Spanish surrender

After the Americans assembled in several rows from right to left according to rank, Shafter presented Toral with the sword and spurs of Brigadier General Vara del Rey, and Toral reciprocated with the Spanish flag. A Spanish bugler sounded a call that brought forth the King's Guard, two hundred strong. Following an exchange of salutes, the officer of the King's Guard marched his column back toward Santiago a few hundred feet, where they stacked arms and retired to the Spanish lines.

Following the surrender, Shafter and Toral, followed by their escorts, rode into Santiago in columns of two to the Plaza de Armas in the center of Santiago, where the cathedral, the governor's palace, the San Carlos Club, and the Café de Venus faced each other on the square.

Whether at religious service (10-52) or at their posts (10-53 and 10-54), enthusiasm prevailed. The Spanish troops seemed to be relieved and fraternized with their American counterparts (10-55). Both sides had developed a respect for each other.

At about 10:00 A.M., the 9th Infantry marched into the square, facing city hall, where thousands were waiting. Reporter Sylvester Scovel of the *New York World* was determined to get to the roof of the city hall for a closeup view of the flag raising. When refused permission, he tried to strike

10-53 Cavalry troopers atop San Juan Hill cheer on receiving the news of the Spanish surrender

10-54 A gathering in the camp of the 2d Infantry on the southern reaches of San Juan Heights following the Spanish surrender.

10-55 Relieved Spanish troops chat with their American counterparts across the trenches.

Shafter—some say he actually did so—and was promptly hustled off to jail, where he remained overnight. On the stroke of noon, the flag was run up as the 9th Infantry band played "The Star-Spangled Banner" (10-56 and 10-57). Throughout the city, Americans and Cubans celebrated (10-58

10-56 With the 9th Infantry in formation in the street below, an honor guard raises the American flag over the city hall of Santiago on July 17 at noon. Note "VIVA ALFONSO XIII" painted just below the roof and the photographer at lower left.

10-57 The Stars and Stripes catches the breeze on its way up the flagstaff as Lieutenant Miley (Shafter's chief aide-de-camp), Captain McKitrick, and Lieutenant Wheeler (General Wheeler's son) stand by on the red-tiled roof.

and 10-59), while the Spanish officers and men performed their last duties with dignity (10-60 and 10-61).

The Americans had taken more prisoners than they expected. To Shafter's surprise, Toral had surrendered all the men under his command, the

10-58 American soldiers line the plaza in front of the cathedral in Santiago on Surrender Day.

10-59 Men of the 9th Infantry in the street below and the Cuban civilians above them share the triumph of the day.

10-60 Spanish officers accompany two U.S. officers, one of whom is almost surely Capt. Lloyd M. Brett, commanding Squadron C, 2d Cavalry, which escorted General Shafter to the Surrender Tree.

10-61 Surrendered Spanish soldiers march out of Santiago under arms.

Military District of Santiago de Cuba, not just the city garrison, so the total was about 22,700. Weapons surrendered included some sixteen thousand rifles and three million rounds of ammunition.

Total American combat casualties in Cuba had been high—243 killed, 1,445 wounded.

There would be more action in Cuba, but for all intents and purposes the war was over.

CHAPTER 11

The United States Acquires an Empire

Hostilities in the Santiago area ceased so abruptly and so completely that the American soldiers may well have felt like a man who has been battering at a door, only to find it unlocked. They were very much interested in examining the Spanish positions such as Fort St. Iñez (11-1). The Americans looking over the barbed-wire entanglements shown in photograph 11-2 no doubt experienced considerable relief that they no longer had to take such formidable emplacements. Construction of the Spanish trench lines surrounding Santiago had begun during April 1898. They were dug deep, with perpendicular sides. Often, all of the excavated dirt was carried far enough away that the works were almost invisible at four to five hundred yards, at which point an enemy was almost irrevocably committed to an advance. Rather less impressive were the defenses of a Spanish blockhouse (11-3) and observation tower (11-4).

Santiago came as a surprise to the Americans. What should have been a beautiful old city was virtually uninhabitable by U.S. standards. To the shock of the Americans, the citizens seemed to have no concept of sanitation. Waste was thrown into the streets or back yards and left to rot. The U.S. Army soon established in Santiago an office of its Sanitary Department (11-5). The Signal Corps set up its headquarters in Santiago (11-6), but as much as possible all soldiers were moved back to the comparative safety of the hills.

The first military governor appointed was Lt. Col. Chambers McKibbin, who was succeeded

11-1 American officers inspect Fort St. Iñez—in reality only a large blockhouse—behind the Spanish siege lines on the northeast outskirts of Santiago.

11-2 After the conclusion of the siege American soldiers in the background at right examine a barbed-wire entanglement fronting a set of Spanish rifle pits.

11-3 A Spanish blockhouse enclosed by a sandbagged parapet, strengthened by numerous traverses

11-4 A fortified Spanish observation tower near Santiago

11-5 The Sanitary Department's office in the city of Santiago

11-6 Santiago headquarters of the U.S. Signal Corps

shortly by Brig. Gen. Leonard Wood. There could not have been a better choice, for Wood was a physician who also had outstanding executive ability. He would need every ounce of his skill. There were 1,800 patients in the Santiago hospital, and every house seemed to have its sick. It was estimated that there were forty thousand people for the Red Cross to feed (11-7). The harbor opened on July 19, and the first ship in was the *State of Texas*, owned and operated by the Red Cross, with Clara Barton on board. They were able to provide food for about 10,000 civilians daily.

There were other problems. The surrender had destroyed the value of Cuban and Spanish money. Only gold was accepted until the value of U.S. currency could be determined. Business had to be restored, order maintained, and the authority of the Americans established.

11-7 Famished Cuban civilians turn out in Santiago for food distributed by the Americans.

The tenuous relationship between the American authorities and the Cuban insurgents had gradually eroded and at this point it collapsed. The only Cubans at the surrender ceremony had been General Joaquin Castillo and an aide—as guests, not participants. The Cubans had raised a flag over Morro, and Sampson had ordered it taken down. The insurgents wanted General Demetrius Castillo to be military governor and recommended him to Shafter, who rejected the proposal. Cuban leaders maintained that at the first meeting between General Calixto García, Sampson, and Shafter, the latter had promised to turn Santiago over to García as soon as it surrendered. This may or may not have been true, but the intervening time had seen a rapid drop in the Americans' regard for the insurgents, who were seen as brave but undisciplined, and Shafter blamed García for the successful Spanish reinforcement of Santiago.

Shafter's motive in freezing out the insurgents is not clear. Perhaps he hesitated to turn them loose in Santiago; perhaps he preferred that peace terms with Spain be a one-on-one settlement without the complication of a third party. Nevertheless, the Cubans had been fighting the Spanish for several years before the Americans arrived on the scene, and their human losses had been higher proportionately than the U.S. losses. What a contemporary historian called "kindly candor" might have defused the situation, but Shafter was a sick man and had a brusque disposition. García collected his men and took off for the hills.

Meanwhile, able-bodied Americans embarked on road-building and improvement projects (11-8 and 11-9) and determining what to do with obso-

11-8 During the occupation of Santiago, the Army embarked on road-building and improvement projects. Seen here is the road leading from Santiago to the San Juan battlefield.

11-9 Road under construction at Boniato near Santiago

lete war matériel (11-10). Unfortunately, in short order the term able-bodied applied to fewer and fewer men. Cases of tropical fevers, especially yellow fever, and malaria, typhoid, and dysentery increased. Secretary Alger refused to permit yellow fever patients to return to the United States. In a very short time, it was estimated that only half of the American troops were fit for duty.

Shafter telegraphed Alger that unless the V Corps and its accompanying regiments were returned immediately to the United States, "the death rate will be appalling." Alger agreed, but before this the generals and Theodore Roosevelt had signed a statement of support for Shafter, which became known as the "Round Robin" because of the multiple signatures. They declared, "This army must be moved at once or it will perish. . . . Persons responsible for preventing such a move will be responsible for the unnecessary loss of many thousands of lives." This was sent on August 3, and the Associated Press leaked it before Alger officially received it, which embarrassed the War Department. Actually, the decision to move the troops had been made the previous day, but in the eyes of the public, the "Round Robin" did no harm to the signers' reputations, especially that of Roosevelt, who was already a popular hero.

About 514 soldiers died of disease in Cuba, as did about half as many aboard transports to Montauk, New York. At Montauk the returnees spent four days in a "detention camp." If no signs of yellow fever developed, they were moved to permanent quarters with "good food and comfortable beds."

During this period, detachments of the army were sent to accept the surrender of the much-dispersed Spanish forces in southeastern Cuba (11-11). For example, Lieutenant Colonel Ewers went to Guantánamo to accept the surrender of the garrison there (11-12). The last of the Spanish forces in Cuba surrendered in August 1898.

11-10 With the surrender of the Spanish forces in and around Santiago, Americans found themselves encumbered with outdated war matériel, such as these smoothbore artillery tubes and shells.

11-11 In the background, Col. Leonard Wood of the Rough Riders raises the American flag at San José de las Lajas after the Spanish capitulation.

11-12 American soldiers raise the American flag at Rowell Barracks in Guantánamo after taking possession on October 4, 1898.

Spanish soldiers were returned home after being held in camps outside Santiago and at Guantánamo. The War Department asked for bids for transporting them, and, ironically, the Spanish Transatlantic Company won. The contract specified adequate rations and no overcrowding. Between August 9 and September 17, 22,864 soldiers were repatriated at a cost of $513,860. Spanish sailors who were held at Portsmouth, New Hampshire, were repatriated by a similar arrangement. One reason the Spanish troops were returned so quickly was Shafter's desire to transport rapidly as many of the Americans guarding them as possible out of the disease-ridden camps and back to the United States (11-13).

This movement homeward of the Spanish soldiers occasioned an incident that may be unique in the annals of war. A Spanish infantry private, Pedro Lopez de Castillo, took a plebiscite among eleven thousand of his fellow soldiers, then wrote to Shafter asking that "all the courageous and noble soldiers under your command may receive our good wishes and farewell. . . ." The accompanying letter, addressed to the "Soldiers of the American Army" sent their opposites' "most cordial and sincere good wishes and farewell." They assured the Americans that they held no resentment "against the men who fought us nobly and valiantly," in contrast to the Cubans, against whom they were very bitter. "You fought us as men, face to face, and with great courage, . . . a quality which we had not met with during the three years we have carried on this war against a people who could not confront the enemy, but hidden, shot their noble victims from ambushes and then immediately fled."

They acknowledged the American contrast—honorable burial of the dead, treatment of the wounded "with great humanity," respect and care for prisoners, the freely given food and medicine. They wished the American soldiers "all happiness and health in Cuba" but added a Parthian shot full of the bitter pride of Spain: ". . . but the descendants of the Congo and of Guinea, mingled with the blood of unscrupulous Spaniards and of traitors and adventurers, these people are not able to exercise or enjoy their liberty, for they will find it a burden to comply with the laws which govern civilized communities."

Some of the higher-ranking prisoners astounded the Americans by the ignorance in which Madrid had kept them. For example, Cervera and his officers learned of Dewey's victory at Manila Bay only after they had been taken prisoner. By the same token, Governor General Augustín of the Philippines had been told that Cervera had annihilated Sampson's ships "and was ravaging the American coasts. . . ."

While matters were winding down in Cuba, action continued elsewhere. On July 18 General Miles received permission to sail for Puerto Rico, which he had been hoping to take. His men, un-

11-13 American troops embark on launches, which will shuttle them out to transports bound for the United States.

like those who were on Cuba, were in good physical condition, having been kept on transports. The fall of Santiago de Cuba and the destruction of Cervera's fleet had reduced Puerto Rico's strategic importance, and Sampson refused to send an armored ship with Miles until McKinley ordered him to do so.

In 1898 Puerto Rico had a population of a little under one million. Politically it was considered an integral part of Spain rather than a colony. Unlike Cuba, it had recently been granted an autonomous government, and there had been little revolutionary activity. Spain had posted 8,233 regulars in Puerto Rico, with 9,107 volunteers.

Gloucester ran ahead of Miles's main body, landing at Guánica near Ponce on July 25. *Gloucester*'s men captured ten lighters and used them to disembark men and supplies. Richard Harding Davis reported that within a few hours two thousand men of the 6th Illinois Volunteer Infantry and the 6th Massachusetts were encamped. During a skirmish the next day, bullets from the overeager 6th Illinois struck Miles's transport and the ship carrying the Red Cross nurses. The latter seemed pleased to be under fire, even if it was what would later be called "friendly fire."

Miles received prompt reinforcements from the mainland. On July 27, Maj. Gen. James H. Wilson arrived with 3,600 men; on July 31, Brig. Gen. Theodore Schwan brought 2,900; and on August 3, Maj. Gen. John R. Brooke landed 5,000. This was much less than Miles had requested, but it was more than enough, especially because the Puerto Rican troops usually chose to desert rather than fight.

The major engagement was on August 9 at Coamo, where the Americans suffered six wounded, with no fatalities. Six Spanish soldiers were killed, including the commandante, and thirty or forty wounded. The Puerto Rico campaign came to an abrupt end on August 12, when the War Department advised Miles that a peace protocol had been signed and that all military operations were to cease immediately.

On the other side of the world, Dewey's spectacular victory at Manila Bay had resulted in a temporary stalemate. His fleet controlled the bay and the surrounding ocean, but the Spanish regulars and militia in Manila outnumbered him almost twenty to one. He could only await reinforcements from the United States, which would take about eight weeks, and hope that the Spanish relief squadron would not arrive first. While he was waiting, the Germans made life interesting. It was customary at the time for major powers to send a warship to a possible trouble scene to observe and report the action and to provide protection to noncombatants. Great Britain, France, Japan, and Germany sent such observers to Manila Bay. The first three nations sent one ship each, but Germany sent six, including the flagship of its Asiatic Squadron, *Kaiserin Augusta*, with Vice Admiral Otto von Diederichs in command. These German "observers" comprised a force at least as strong as Dewey's. They were certainly annoying, moving in and out of the bay at will and demonstrating friendly respect for the Spanish. Dewey was suspicious of their intentions, but there was no evidence that they were there to interfere with the Americans.

The Spanish on land were having troubles with Emilio Aguinaldo and his insurgents. By June 12, Aguinaldo proclaimed Philippine independence and eleven days later announced the formation of a provisional government under his presidency.

An American expeditionary force was being gathered at San Francisco under the command of Maj. Gen. Wesley Merritt, who, except for Miles, was the U.S. Army's senior ranking general. He was under orders to join Dewey and capture Manila. His instruction was "giving order and security to the island." The singular noun "island" left vague whether the target was the entire Philippine archipelago or only Luzon. Because of a shortage of transport, the expedition moved in three separate convoys. Brig. Gen. Thomas M. Anderson, with approximately 2,500 men sailed on May 25. On June 15 the second group of 3,500 sailed under Brig. Gen. Thomas M. Andrews. From June 25 to 29, the third increment of some 5,000, with Merritt on board, departed under the command of Brig. Gen. Arthur MacArthur, whose son Douglas was to outshine his father in later years. The total of 407 officers and 10,437 men was more than twice what Dewey had requested.

While this expedition was under way, almost as an afterthought the United States annexed the Hawaiian Islands, a move it had contemplated for years. With the war moving into the Pacific, it was obvious that the United States would need naval bases in that ocean. McKinley signed a joint resolution on July 7, and the Hawaiian Islands were annexed on August 12, 1898.

The three convoys of troops reached Manila between June 3 and August 7. On August 7, Dewey gave the Spanish governor general, Fermin Juadenes, forty-eight hours' notice of his intention to bombard Manila. Juadenes was reluctant to surrender without a fight, but was even more reluctant to fall to the insurgents. Dewey and Merritt took the decision out of his hands by attacking on August 13. They planned a relatively bloodless battle and decided to keep Aguinaldo's men, as García's men had been at Santiago, out of the city. The attack was all over by 5:43 P.M., when the American flag was raised. Actually this peculiar battle had been unnecessary; a peace protocol had already been signed in Washington on August 12, but because of communication problems word did not reach Manila until August 16.

The peace process began on July 18 when Spain's foreign minister, the Duke of Almodóvar del Río, asked the French government in Paris to authorize Jules-Martin Cambon, French ambassador to Washington, to act as intermediary between Washington and Madrid. The French complied, and Spain gave Cambon full powers to negotiate. He met with McKinley and Secretary of State William Day on July 26, and on July 30 the president gave Cambon his reply. Spain must give up Cuba and evacuate its military immediately. Spain also must cede Puerto Rico and one of the Ladrones, probably Guam, and would receive "a financial indemnity." The United States would occupy Manila pending the forthcoming peace conference.

Spain had little choice but to accept; however, it had centuries of experience in diplomatic maneuvering and tried a number of ploys to keep the demand limited to Cuba. But McKinley was inflexible. Cambon and the president signed the protocol at 4:30 P.M. on August 12.

Before the formal peace conference, evacuation of Puerto Rico and Cuba was arranged. The latter task proved time consuming and was not completed until January 1, 1899 (11-14). The first meeting of the peace conference was held in Paris, at the French Foreign Office. The protocol had been difficult for the Spanish to accept, and no

11-14 Transfer of authority to the Americans at Pinar del Rio on January 1, 1899

Conservative Party member would agree to serve in Spain's delegation. The Spanish instead sent three liberals—Eugenio Montero Rios, who served as president; Buenaventura de Abarzuza y Ferrer; José de Garnica y Díaz; diplomat Wenceslao Ramirez de Villaurrutia y Villaurrutia; and General Rafael Cerero y Sáenz.

For the United States, Day resigned as secretary of state in order to serve as chairman. His colleagues were three expansionist Republicans—Whitelaw Reid, a former ambassador to France and publisher of the New York *Tribune*; Senators Cushman K. Davis of Minnesota and William P. Frye of Maine—and one distinguished Democrat and isolationist, Senator George Gray of Delaware (11-15). There was no representative from Cuba, Puerto Rico, or the Philippines.

As expected, negotiations dragged on, but the results were inevitable. Spain relinquished its sovereignty over Cuba and ceded Puerto Rico, Guam, and the Philippines, while the United States agreed to pay Spain $20,000,000 for the latter. The treaty was signed on December 10, 1898, and went to the respective governments for ratification. The U.S. Senate ratified the treaty on February 6, 1899, after what Lodge wrote to Roosevelt was "the closest, hardest fight I have ever known." Spain waited until the United States had ratified before acting on the treaty. Spaniards in general seemed to bear no malice toward the Americans and appeared relieved that the war had ended and Spain had been freed from the crushing financial and personnel cost of maintaining reluctant colonies. But the Cortes floundered in a morass of political ramifications. Finally, on March 6, 1899, Queen Regent María Cristina lost patience and closed the Cortes. She personally signed the treaty on March 19. The war officially ended on April 11 with the exchange of ratifications.

11-15 The final session of the Spanish American Peace Commission in Paris, December 10, 1898. Attendees (left to right) are: Senator William P. Frye; Secretary John B. Moore; Senator George Gray; Secretary Cushman K. Davis; Judge William R. Day; Hon. Whitelaw Reid; General Rafael Cerero y Síenz; Señor W. R. de Villaurrutia y Villaurrutia; Señor José Garnica; Señor B. de Abarzuza; Señor Montero Rios; interpreter Ferguson; and Sec. Emilio de Ojeda.

CHAPTER 12

Aftermath

"'Take what you want—and pay for it,' says God" is an old Spanish proverb. The Americans had taken what they wanted and for a time seemed to be paying a remarkably small price. The first instinct of the American people was to celebrate and memorialize. So many tried to chip souvenirs off the cottonwood Surrender Tree that it had to be fenced off (12-1).

On August 20, 1898, just eight days after the peace protocol was signed, a fleet review was held at New York City, featuring Sampson's flagship, *New York*, with *Iowa*, *Oregon*, and *Brooklyn* (12-2). "The fleet received a magnificent reception," wrote Naval Cadet Cyrus R. Miller from his vantage point on board *Oregon*, "all along the river, crowded craft saluting with shrieking sirens without cessation. Saw many beautiful women thanks to a good pair of glasses."

Less than a month later, September 16, the 1st Marine Battalion marched through Portsmouth, New Hampshire (12-3), after which the leathernecks feasted on a "meal never to be forgotten," replete with, among other items, forty-eight bushels of clams, 2,500 "good large lobsters," a thousand ears of corn, six barrels of sweet potatoes, rolls, bread, crackers, pickles, and watermelon, washed down with one hundred gallons of "very fine coffee" and fifty cases of beer.

At roughly the same time—September 1898—Spanish naval prisoners of war, including Admiral Cervera (12-4) and prisoners hospitalized at Portsmouth, New Hampshire (12-5), were preparing to return to Spain aboard the steamship *City of Rome* (12-6). Aside from their natural disappointment in having been defeated, they, like their army colleagues who departed from Cuba, had little of which to complain. Cervera and his fellow officers had been treated as welcome guests rather than as prisoners, and the enlisted men had received the best care available.

12-1 The Surrender Tree, seen here after the event, as it lies surrounded by a fence to discourage overzealous souvenir hunters

12-2 Rear Admiral Sampson's flagship, the armored cruiser *New York*, leads the battleships *Iowa* and *Oregon* and (behind *Oregon*) the armored cruiser *Brooklyn* in the fleet review at New York City, August 20, 1898.

12-3 The 1st Marine Battalion marches triumphantly through Portsmouth, New Hampshire, September 16, 1898.

12-4 Admiral Cervera (right), a prisoner of war, walks ashore at Portsmouth, New Hampshire, accompanied by a U.S. naval officer.

12-5 Hospitalized Spanish prisoners of war, Portsmouth, New Hampshire

12-6 The steamship *City of Rome*, seen here off Kittery Point, Maine, transported former Spanish prisoners of war back to Spain in September 1898.

Over a period of time, various acts of respect and remembrance took place. Those Americans who fell in the Santiago campaign were disinterred and reburied in Arlington National Cemetery (12-7). Those who lost their lives during the first battle in Cuba, Las Guásimas, were remembered with an obelisk at Sevilla (12-8). Those lost at San Juan Heights were remembered (12-9), as were victims of Spain who perished before the Spanish-American War (12-10). Cuba also honored its martyrs (12-11). Dewey's flagship, *Olympia*, commemorated the Battle of Manila Bay with a plaque (12-12). Hometown heroes were honored across America. For example, a statue of Ens. Worth Bagley, a native son who died during the attack on Cardenas, was erected on Capitol Square in Raleigh, North Carolina (12-13).

Salvage efforts in Cuban waters began promptly. The Spanish had scuttled the gunboat *Sandoval* at Guantánamo, but on July 14, 1898, U.S. forces seized her. They raised her on August 30 of that year (12-14), and she remained on the U.S. naval vessel register until 1919, when the navy sold her, and she became a private yacht.

General Toral had intended to sink the Spanish cruiser *Reina Mercedes* in the channel at Santiago on July 4, 1898, an effort that proved unsuccessful. In March 1899, she was refloated (12-15), then towed to Norfolk, Virginia, where she became a receiving ship. Later she served as a receiving ship

at the Naval Academy until 1957. Efforts to save *Infanta María Teresa* ended in dismal failure, and she was abandoned in November 1898.

Then came the ship raising that really interested the American people. In the late spring of 1911, work began to float *Maine* to clear Havana harbor. By early June the cofferdam construction had been completed and pumping had begun (12-16). On June 16, the vessel's upperworks broke the surface (12-17).

By March 16, 1912, the battleship was ready to be towed out to sea (12-18), as interested crowds looked on (12-19). At 5:21 P.M. on that day, *Maine* was scuttled some four miles off the coast of Cuba (12-20). Only two significant relics were recovered from the wreck—her foremast, which went to the Naval Academy, and her mainmast, which is in Arlington National Cemetery. For some time, it was still believed that the Spanish had sunk *Maine*, and periodically her memory was honored (12-21). Later examination of various data and testimony in 1911 proved no more conclusive than the first inquiry in 1898.

Oddly enough, the chief cost to the United States came not from Cuba, the center of attention, but from the Philippines. Furiously angry and disappointed at what they considered the American betrayal, Aguinaldo and his insurgents fought the United States from February 4, 1899, until July 1902. This Philippine insurrection cost the United

12-7 U.S. dead from the Santiago Campaign are brought home for burial at Arlington National Cemetery.

12-8 The U.S. Army erected a simple obelisk adjacent to the old sundial at Sevilla as a memorial to those who lost their lives during the campaign's first battle at Las Guásimas.

12-9 Memorial to the Americans who gave their lives on San Juan Heights

12-10 Memorial plaque erected to the memory of the slain *Virginius* prisoners

12-11 Shrine to Cuban dead, Havana

States more than 4,200 soldiers killed. The Filipinos lost about 20,000 soldiers and ten times as many civilians. Until July 4, 1946, Philippine Independence Day, Aguinaldo wore a black bow tie to symbolize mourning for the Philippine Republic. He then removed the tie, basking in the knowledge that at last the Philippines were truly free. He died on February 6, 1964, at the age of ninety-four.

Cuba never became an American possession but was in effect a protectorate for many years. The last remnant of that period is a lease on Guantánamo as a U.S. naval station.

For such a short war, and one so localized between two major combatants, the Spanish-American War had far-reaching effects. To be sure, Spain had been fighting the Cuban insurgents for many years before the United States entered the conflict, and at one time about 50 percent of its army was engaged in Cuba. All told, Spain lost approximately fifty thousand men, bankrupted the home country, and lost most of its remaining overseas empire. Because its culture had held the military in high esteem, such a decisive defeat at the hands of what many Europeans regarded as a money-grubbing upstart was a crushing blow to

Spanish national pride. Perhaps it was only natural that the Spanish should blame their own army and navy more bitterly than they did the United States.

In a way, Spain profited by losing the war. In no other way would its grip on Cuba, Guam, and the Philippines have been loosened, and thus it probably would have continued to pour its treasure and its best young men into a lost cause. Instead, it

12-12 Plaque affixed to the face of the protected cruiser *Olympia*'s forward turret, circa 1900, commemorating the Battle of Manila Bay.

12-13 Statue of Ens. Worth Bagley erected on Capitol Square in Raleigh, North Carolina.

could now turn its energies and gifts into improving the homeland. There would be difficult times, but in due course Spain would fulfill its own "manifest destiny" as a respected member of the European Community.

In contrast, the United States inherited numerous troubles. On the credit side for the United States, service together in a common cause had done much to heal the wounds of the Civil War. Much of Europe entertained a heightened re-

12-14 Salvagers raise the sunken Spanish gunboat *Sandoval* at Guantánamo Bay, August 30, 1898.

12-15 Salvaging the Spanish cruiser *Reina Mercedes* at Santiago, with Merritt's wrecking organization schooner *F. R. Sharp* alongside.

spect for the United States as an undeniable, if not exactly welcome, player on the world stage. On the debit side, however, some Europeans had exchanged their contempt or indifference for something like real fear and spoke of the "American peril" as a later generation of Americans would speak of the "yellow peril" or "red menace." Relations improved significantly with Great Britain,

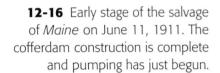 **12-16** Early stage of the salvage of *Maine* on June 11, 1911. The cofferdam construction is complete and pumping has just begun.

12-17 Pumping proceeds on June 16 as the vessel's upperworks break the surface of the water.

which had more or less openly sided with the United States. To those of Theodore Roosevelt's thinking, results of the war were "bully."

Others were not so sure. Many Americans were deeply suspicious of imperialism and of a potent military force. Although relations with Europe had improved, those with Latin America had deteriorated. Most Latin Americans sympathized with the Cuban rebels, but at the same time sided with the Spanish instead of the Americans. If one were going to be pushed around, better to keep it in the family. Those erstwhile allies of the Americans, the Cuban and Filipino insurgents, were furious at being, in their eyes, betrayed. Instead of becoming independent, they had just exchanged one colonial power for another.

12-18 Now afloat, *Maine* stands ready to be towed out to sea on March 16, 1912.

12-19 March 16, 1912. A fascinated crowd watches as tugs tow out to sea the symbol of American indignation that led to the Spanish-American War.

Both Cuba and the Philippines presented early and difficult questions for which there were no immediate answers. Amazingly few in the U.S. government had given serious consideration to the question, "What comes next?" There were no carefully thought-out plans as to how to deal with these uncomfortable new responsibilities.

Especially troublesome were the Philippines, because their guardianship made the United States an Asiatic power. The Americans had been involved in Asia for some years but not as a permanent resident of the area. It has been suggested

that, although many other factors were involved, out of the Spanish-American War came the United States' participation in World War II in the Pacific. Had the United States not been a formidable presence in the Philippines, Guam, and Hawaii, the Japanese would have had no strategic reason to attack.

The United States made many blunders in dealing with Cuba and the Philippines, but the fact remains that today they are independent nations, thanks at least in part to that strange little conflict, the Spanish-American War.

12-20 At 5:21 P.M., March 16, amid great ceremony, *Maine* slips beneath the waves four miles off the coast of Cuba in six hundred fathoms of water.

12-21 Ceremonies at the monument honoring the battleship *Maine* at Havana, photographed in the late 1920s. In the foreground are some of the firemen who carried the dead to the cemetery in 1898.

Index

Page numbers in italics refer to illustrations and their captions.
Unless otherwise noted, military units refer to U.S. units.

The Authors

Donald M. Goldstein teaches public and international affairs at the University of Pittsburgh. With **Katherine V. Dillon** and the late Gordon W. Prange, he created the World War II classics *At Dawn We Slept*; *Miracle at Midway*; *December 7, 1941*; *Pearl Harbor: The Verdict of History*; *Target Tokyo*; and *God's Samurai: Lead Pilot at Pearl Harbor*. More recently they worked together on *Amelia: The Centennial Biography of an Aviation Pioneer*. Historian **J. Michael Wenger** collaborated with Dr. Goldstein and Ms. Dillon on *The Way It Was— Pearl Harbor: The Original Photographs*; *D-Day Normandy: The Story and Photographs*; *Nuts! The Battle of the Bulge: The Story and Photographs*; and *Rain of Ruin: A Photographic History of Hiroshima and Nagasaki*. The author of several books on naval history topics, **Robert J. Cressman** is a historian at the Naval Historical Center in Washington, D.C.